THE GREAT LIVES SERIES

Here are the life stories of courageous men and women from all walks of life, in every corner of the globe, who have challenged the way society thinks, stood up for their rights, and changed the world. Whether fighting for racial, social, or economic justice and freedom, these history makers have won victories that were once thought to be impossible, and have inspired hope when all were hopeless. They can still teach all of us unforgettable lessons by the very fact of their great lives.

Other biographies in the Great Lives Series

GREAT LIVES
MALCOLM X
A Force for Change

Nikki Grimes

FAWCETT COLUMBINE
NEW YORK

For middle-school readers

A Fawcett Columbine Book
Published by Ballantine Books

Library of Congress Catalog Card Number: 92-90414

ISBN 0-449-90803-8

Cover design by Georgia Morrissey

Cover illustration by Ann Meisel

Manufactured in the United States of America

First Edition: November 1992

10 9 8 7 6 5 4 3 2

TABLE OF CONTENTS

MALCOLM X

Malcolm addresses a street crowd at 125th Street and 7th Avenue in the heart of Harlem. Circa 1962.

PHOTO BY ROBERT L. HAGGINS

1

In the Eye of the Storm

LOUD MUSIC FROM a jukebox spilled out of a bar on Lenox Avenue one warm spring night in Harlem, New York. Slick hustlers with processed hair swarmed up and down the avenue in sharkskin suits, selling "hot" watches and radios while drug dealers traded bags of heroine and cocaine for cash. Dope addicts nodded against corner lampposts, barely responding to the wail of police and ambulance sirens that now and then pierced the air. The streets were littered with empty beer cans and broken whiskey bottles, but the hustlers and addicts certainly didn't care.

There was one spot in the neighborhood, though, that was particularly clean and well kept, and that was Nation of Islam Temple Number Seven. The sidewalk in front of the temple and the adjoining restaurant on West 116th Street was swept daily and kept litter free, and the atmosphere inside was peaceful. The men and women within spoke in moderate voices, doing nothing to compete with the commotion beyond the temple doors. Perhaps that's why few people in Harlem paid much attention to the temple or to the

1

steadily growing numbers of Muslims within the community. But that was all about to change.

A few blocks from the temple, two white police officers broke up a street fight. "All right! Move it!" they said, ordering the bystanders to leave. Among the crowd were two Muslims from Temple Number Seven. They were very dignified young men, and refused to scatter as quickly and fearfully as the other blacks, or "Negroes" as they were known in those days. This made the policemen furious. Without warning, they turned on a young man named Johnson Hinton and beat him with their billy clubs. By the time they stopped, Hinton's scalp was split open and his head was bathed in blood. A police car pulled up and took the bleeding man to a local precinct. Hinton's companion found the nearest telephone and called the restaurant, knowing that Temple Seven officials would be there.

Malcolm X, minister of Temple Number Seven, was in the temple's restaurant when the call came in. When he heard the news, he gritted his teeth but responded calmly. He knew there was no point expressing his anger. This was not the first time white policemen had brutalized an innocent black man. Such occurrences were far too common. But then, as the Honorable Elijah Muhammad had taught him, the black man could not expect just or humane treatment at the hands of a white man, because the white man was the devil. A lifetime of harsh experiences had prepared Malcolm to accept that teaching as fact. According to rumors in the Lansing, Michigan, community where Malcolm spent his early childhood, his own father had been killed by white racists.

And, though the year was now 1957, a white racist group called the Ku Klux Klan still lynched blacks in the South. Johnson Hinton's beating was just the latest in a long line of white crimes committed against the black man.

But this time would be different. This time the parties responsible would be made to account for their crimes. Malcolm X and the Nation of Islam would see to that.

Harnessing his anger, Malcolm took the situation in hand. He saw to it that several calls were placed during the next quarter-hour. Shortly thereafter, fifty men from Temple Seven, members of the Nation of Islam's honor guard, the Fruit of Islam, met and formed tight ranks outside of the police precinct where Johnson Hinton was being held. A steadily growing black crowd of local residents and curious passersby gathered behind them. When police looked outside and saw the crowd, and the tall, stern-faced, red-haired black man in the lead, they became nervous.

Malcolm strode into the station and demanded to see "Brother Hinton." At first he was told that Hinton was not there, but when pressed, police finally admitted to Hinton's presence and led Malcolm to the holding cell. Malcolm was sickened by the sight of his Muslim brother beaten and bloodied. "That man belongs in the hospital," he told the lieutenant in charge. Sensing trouble, the officer immediately called for an ambulance, which took Hinton to nearby Harlem Hospital.

Malcolm led the stone-faced, disciplined Muslim group through the streets of Harlem directly to Harlem Hospital. Malcolm knew those streets better than anyone. He'd hustled his way through those streets dealing in drugs and stolen goods once himself. But Elijah Muhammad, who he'd come to worship, had saved him from that life. Now Malcolm was committed to doing the same for others.

As these clean-shaven, well-dressed, and clearly determined young men marched along Lenox Avenue, a large and angry-looking crowd formed behind them. They, too, were tired of police brutality, and they were eager to see how this organized group of black men would confront it. When they reached the hospital, Malcolm and his followers took up silent vigil out front.

A police official approached Malcolm. "Get those people out of there," he ordered. But Malcolm eyed the man levelly and stood his ground. Malcolm pointed out that his people were gathering in a peaceful and disciplined manner, disturbing no one. The official noted that the angry crowd behind Malcolm's group wasn't so disciplined. "Those people are your problem—not mine," Malcolm told him politely. His comment did nothing to ease the tension.

Just as the strain of the situation became unbearable, a Harlem Hospital doctor came out to assure Malcolm that Johnson Hinton was receiving the best care available. Satisfied, Malcolm gave the word and his followers quietly disappeared into the night. Following their lead, the rest of the crowd scattered.

The incident made headlines in the black-owned *Amsterdam News* the next day, but by the time the paper hit the newsstands, Harlem was already buzzing. *Who are those Muslims?* everybody wanted to know. Within the coming months and years, people across America and around the world would be asking the same question. And if anyone was ready to give the answer, it was Malcolm X. He was the most devoted follower and most articulate spokesman for Elijah Muhammad and the Nation of Islam.

Established in 1930 by Elijah Muhammad, the Nation of Islam is a religious organization loosely based on the religion of Islam, which is practiced in the Arab world. Muhammad learned this new version of Islam from a traveling preacher named W. D. Fard. Fard called himself "The Prophet." According to Elijah, Fard taught him that Allah, the one true God, is black, and that Allah had chosen Elijah to be "His last messenger" to U.S. blacks, who were the "lost sheep of North America." Fard reportedly disappeared in 1934, leaving Muhammad head of the new Nation.

Elijah Muhammad told his followers that white people were a race of devils who were evil by nature. He insisted that the black man was superior, that the black man was, in fact, a god. This was the most shocking idea by far. Up until this time, only members of the white race had ever claimed to be superior. And, since America was a country in which black people still had to fight for equal rights, the idea of black superiority was outrageous. Finally, Muhammad taught that the only true solution to the race problem in America was the complete economic, social, and political separation of the races.

Such teaching was quite a contrast to the ideology of supporters of the Civil Rights Movement, which was gaining momentum at the time. Leaders like Martin Luther King, Jr., Ralph Abernathy, and members of the Congress Of Racial Equality and the Student Non-

Violent Coordinating Committee were risking life and limb pushing for full integration in both the northern and southern states. These leaders, whom Malcolm referred to as "integration-happy Negroes," found Elijah Muhammad's teachings explosive. As far as they were concerned, such teachings did nothing but set back the cause of American blacks.

Malcolm X, born Malcolm Little, was in Concord Prison serving time for burglary when he first heard Elijah Muhammad's message. It was a hard message to accept at first. But as he learned about the rich and glorious history of his African forebears, and realized that the truth of his identity had been kept from him by the white man, and as he weighed the injustices that the white man had committed against his people for centuries, the teachings of Muhammad struck a chord. Over time, Malcolm developed a strong sense of race pride, as well as a sense of remorse for the crimes he'd committed against his black brothers and sisters during his years as a street hustler called "Detroit Red."

Elijah Muhammad's new and radical teachings changed the course of Malcolm's life. Once he was out of prison, he spread that teaching more energetically than any other Muslim. By 1957, the Nation had temples in Detroit, Chicago, Boston, Hartford, Springfield, Atlanta, and Philadelphia as well as New York, and many of these temples were established through Malcolm's own tireless recruiting campaigns. Little wonder that Elijah named him minister of the critically based Temple Seven in the heart of Harlem—America's most influential black community.

That is how he came to be in the temple's restaurant on that mild spring night in 1957 when the phone call came in about Johnson Hinton. That incident, and Malcolm's handling of it, would help put the Nation of Islam on the map. Soon thereafter, the telephone in Nation of Islam Temple Number Seven would be ringing constantly as reporters from around the world called to ask the "fiery chief of the Black Muslims" why he taught "black supremacy and hate."

As Malcolm drove home that April evening, he could hardly have guessed that Temple Number Seven would so soon become the focus of national controversy, and that he would be in the eye of the storm!

He was up to the challenge, though. That was clear from his earliest days in the Nation. In a public address he gave in Detroit—one of his first—he'd looked out at the upturned faces of seventy-five to one hundred brother and sister Muslims before him and said: "I have sat at the Messenger's feet hearing the truth from his own mouth! I have pledged on my knees to Allah to tell the white man about his crimes and the black man the true teachings of our Honorable Elijah Muhammad. I don't care if it costs me my life. . . . "

The course he had set for himself would, indeed, cost Malcolm his life. But first, there was work to be done. There was a nation of blacks to be awakened. There was a spirit of black pride to be spread abroad. There was a white nation to be called to account for its crimes. And finally, there was a new vision of universal brotherhood yet to be revealed at the end of this man's journey. It was a vision of people of all races united by faith in the Muslim god, living as one, wor-

7

shiping as one—a vision born in the Muslim Holy Land of Mecca.

Who were those Black Muslims exactly? Soon all the world would know. And who was this Malcolm X? A man to be watched, a voice to be heard, and a force to be reckoned with.

2

In Garvey's Shadow

ONE NIGHT IN December 1924, when Louise Little was four months pregnant with her fourth child, members of the Ku Klux Klan, a white supremacy group, galloped up to her house in Omaha, Nebraska, wearing white hoods, waving torches, and screaming for her husband to come out and show himself. Louise ignored the heavy pounding of her heart and went to the front door. In a calm voice, she told the angry white-robed men that her husband, Earl, was not at home. She said that she was home alone with three small children, and stood so that they could see her swollen belly. Furious that they had missed Earl, they circled the house several times, shoving their gun butts through window after window until shards of glass littered the yard. Finally, the hooded figures galloped off into the night, their flaming torches lighting the path before them.

Louise told her husband of the Klan's unexpected visit when he returned home from a business trip. Enraged, Earl decided to relocate the family as soon as the new baby came and was old enough to withstand the move. When that baby was finally born five months later, it was a red-faced, red-haired little boy. They decided to name him Malcolm.

In the years to come, Malcolm would face down many men like the Klan members his mother had faced that night. He was destined both for greatness and controversy. Of course, the Littles were no strangers to controversy themselves. Everything about who they were and how they lived their lives made them stand out.

Louise Norton and the Reverend Earl Little must have seemed a particularly odd couple when they met in 1919. Earl, a Baptist minister, was a six-foot-four ebony-skinned black man from Reynolds, Georgia, who'd dropped out of elementary school. In contrast, Louise was a small light-skinned woman with straight black hair who could easily have passed for white. She was a mulatto, born in Grenada, British West Indies, to a black mother and a white father whom she'd never met, and she was highly educated. Perhaps their obvious differences attracted Earl and Louise to each other. For whatever reason, the two were wed that same year and moved to Philadelphia, Pennsylvania, where they gave birth to Wilfred, their first son. Within a few years, the family migrated to Omaha, Nebraska, where Louise gave birth to Hilda, Philbert, and Malcolm, in that order.

In the 1920s, when the Littles were beginning their family, segregation was an accepted way of life in America. For the most part, blacks, called Negroes in those days, were forced to live in separate neighborhoods from whites, attend separate schools, and even worship in separate churches. There were integrated neighborhoods in the northern states, but only a few.

And even there, blacks were expected to "know their place" and to be seen and not heard, as though they were children. Indeed, many white descendants of slave owners thought of blacks as just that—children who should speak only when spoken to. Consequently, they had little use for outspoken blacks such as Marcus Aurelius Garvey—a black nationalist of the 1920s—or for the Reverend Earl Little, Malcolm's father. Earl was one of Garvey's followers and key organizers. It was his work for Garvey that led the Ku Klux Klan to chase Earl and his family from one town to another.

Garvey, a proud black man from the British West Indies, had no intention of accepting segregation as a way of life. He believed in neither segregation (the forced separation of people of different races), nor integration (which unites people of different races into a single organization or society). He was aware of the rich and glorious past blacks could lay claim to through their African ancestry—a past that included the glorious kingdoms of Mali and Ghana and the vast and powerful empire of the Black Moors. He knew that blacks were more than equal to whites, and, therefore, encouraged his people to be proud of their race. He preached Negro self-improvement, self-reliance, and economic independence. According to Garvey, the Negro "must strike out for . . . [himself] in the course of material achievement. . . . It is the slave spirit of dependence," asserted Garvey, "that causes our so-called leading men to seek the shelter, leadership, protection and patronage of 'the master.' . . ." Garvey refused to fall into this camp. He proposed that the blacks in America and the West Indies separate themselves from whites completely by returning to the African "homeland."

On the surface, Garvey's idea seemed like a logical, and even desirable, solution to the problem of segregation in America. If whites did not wish to have blacks living with them, why shouldn't the blacks separate from the whites altogether? However, while whites had no desire to live with blacks or embrace them as equals, they *had* grown used to having blacks as servants during slavery, and had become dependent on blacks as a source of cheap, unskilled labor in the years since Abraham Lincoln had signed the Emancipation Proclamation, bringing an end to slavery in America. The fact that Garvey so much as suggested that the whites might lose *their* Negroes made him one of the most hated men in America.

In 1920 Garvey founded an organization called U.N.I.A., or Universal Negro Improvement Association, dedicated to spreading his radical message. He attracted church leaders like Earl Little, and local politicians from among the black working class.

The white supremacist group known as the Ku Klux Klan, or KKK, was none too fond of Marcus Garvey and his U.N.I.A. They hated the fact that the Garveyites were "stirring up their niggers" with talk of race pride and a "back to Africa" movement. In fact, Garvey followers were frequently harassed and run out of town by Klan members wherever they went. Earl Little and his family had been harassed more times than he or his wife Louise could count. Nevertheless, Louise wholeheartedly supported her husband's work for U.N.I.A. The fact that her own father was white was a source of great shame to her. While other blacks envied her fair complexion and "good" straight black hair, Louise preferred darker skin and kinky hair. The prospect of taking part in a black exodus to go live in an African state, occupied and ruled by people of dark complexion, wholly apart from whites—as Garvey advocated—was an idea which suited Louise just fine. Consequently, she was thoroughly prepared to support Earl's efforts to spread the word, no matter what the cost. Even so, there were several encounters with Klansmen that left her shaken and more than a little afraid for her husband and children.

One such incident was the visit from Klansmen just prior to Malcolm's birth. Had Earl been there that night, he might not have lived long enough to hold baby Malcolm in his arms.

On May 19, 1925, in University Hospital in Omaha, Malcolm Little entered the world, kicking and screaming. He was his father's seventh child. Earl had three children from an earlier marriage, all of whom lived in Boston. They were Ella, Earl, Jr., and Mary. Earl's second marriage to Louise produced a total of eight children.

In the same year that Malcolm was born, Garvey was imprisoned for mail fraud. He promised his followers that he would return to lead the movement, but was eventually deported. His disciples never lost faith in him, though, and men like Earl Little were quick to take up the leadership of the fragmented movement.

The Littles remained in Omaha until December 1926, then moved to Milwaukee, Wisconsin, where Malcolm's younger brother Reginald was born. They didn't stay in Wisconsin for very long. U.N.I.A. organizers were no more popular there than they had been in Nebraska. In addition, Earl was determined to find a place where he and his family could grow their own food, save money for a business, and eventually become financially self-reliant, as U. N. I. A. encouraged its followers to do. So in January of 1927, the Littles packed up once again. This time, they headed for Lansing, Michigan, where Earl had bought a house and hoped someday to open his own store.

The new house was to be the Little home for more than two years. By now, Earl and Louise had five children. A sixth child, Yvonne, would be born there.

In the years that followed, Earl continued to devote himself to the care of his family, the preaching of the gospel, and the spreading of Garvey's message. It became difficult to separate his preaching from his teaching, though. His religious sermons began to reflect his nationalist thinking. Influenced by fellow Garveyite Rev. George Alexander McGuire, Earl began to urge his followers to reject white gods, and begin to see God in their own, black image. McGuire suggested that black artists supply a black Christ and a black Madonna for the "proper training" of black children. These ideas became part of Earl's new religious belief system.

As had happened in both Nebraska and Wisconsin, Earl and other U.N.I.A. organizers were routinely harassed and threatened by local white supremacist groups. These men were not all talk and no action, either. They occasionally made good on their threats, a fact Malcolm was to learn very early in life.

One night, in November of 1929, young Malcolm awakened to the sound of shouting and the blast of gunshots. Earl chased two white men off his property with a pistol he kept close by, but he was too late. The men had already set fire to the house. Earl ran inside to save his family as flames licked the walls of the house and thick smoke quickly filled its rooms. Malcolm and the other children were snatched from their beds and frantically rushed out to the front yard, screaming and crying and bumping into one another in the dark. Louise, cradling a newborn in her arms, barely escaped before the walls of the house caved in. The children gathered on the lawn, shivering in their underwear and trembling in fear, clinging to their mother's nightshirt as white policemen and firemen stood idly by and watched the Little home burn to the ground. The orange flames burned their way into Malcolm's memory, and the sight of black plumes of smoke rising into the night sky was one he would never forget.

The police seemed disinterested in the fire itself. However, they were more than a little curious about the pistol that Earl had used to chase the arsonists off his property. Like most men living in rural areas in those days, Malcolm's father kept a .22 rifle and a shotgun in the house for hunting rabbit and other game, but he had no permit for the pistol he'd used that night. The police were eager to find it, but they never succeeded. Earl had managed to hide the gun. Weeks later, Louise sewed the gun inside a pillow.

There wasn't much left to salvage from the fire. Close friends of the family clothed and housed the Littles temporarily. After several weeks, Earl moved his brood to a house on the outskirts of East Lansing.

They didn't remain there long, however, because blacks weren't allowed within the city boundaries after dark. So, in December 1929, Earl built a four-room house in a rural area two miles outside of town. There the family settled for more than nine years—their longest time ever in one place. Louise's last two children, Wesley and Robert, were born there. As for Malcolm, most of his early childhood memories were connected with that house.

Life in East Lansing was fairly simple. The four-room house that Earl built with his own hands was pretty crowded with two adults and, eventually, eight small children. But outside was a child's paradise. There were trees to climb, grass to roll in, and a large garden where the Littles grew most of their own vegetables. Malcolm was even allowed to plant a small garden of his own where he grew peas and other vegetables. "I would patrol the rows on my hands and knees for any worms or bugs," said Malcolm. "I was proud when we had [peas] on our table." Malcolm was also pleased when Louise served chicken (from their own chicken coop). Malcolm's father frequently brought home baby chicks, which Malcolm's mother raised. She raised rabbits as well, but sold them to local white families. Garvey would have been proud of the Littles. They were wonderful models of "Negro self-reliance."

While life was simple and orderly, it was not often peaceful. Malcolm's parents always seemed to be at odds. For one thing, Louise did not want her children eating pork, rabbit, or the other kinds of "soul food" that her southern-born husband insisted on eating. Being equally stubborn, the two fought frequently and fiercely. Sometimes Earl hit his wife. Even when Louise and Earl weren't arguing, Malcolm remembered days when his parents refused to speak to each other. As for the children, Earl severely beat the older ones whenever they broke one of his rules—and he had lots of rules.

The only child to escape Earl's wrath was Malcolm. Unlike the others, Malcolm was usually spanked by his mother. Malcolm often thought that she was especially hard on him. It seemed to Malcolm that his father favored him because of his light coloring, while his mother seemed to favor the darker children, and liked Malcolm the least. He once remarked that, on sunny days, his mother was forever pushing him out of the house so that he could "get some color."

In general, though, daily life for the Littles continued much as it had in Nebraska and Wisconsin. Louise cared for the home and the children while Earl conducted God's business on Sunday, and Garvey's business the rest of the week. He never had a church of his own, but was always the visiting preacher at various local Baptist churches. The U.N.I.A. meetings he organized were quietly held in the homes of local blacks, despite regular threats from the Black Legion, a local white supremacist group. They were much like the KKK, except that they dressed in black robes and hoods, rather than white.

Malcolm sensed that his father did special work, something that had more to do with those private meetings than with the fiery sermons he gave in church on Sunday mornings. "As young as I was then," Malcolm later wrote, "I knew from what I overheard that my father was saying something that made him a 'tough' man. I remember an old lady grinning and saying to my father, 'You're scaring these white folks to death!' '' The fact that Earl was a strapping, muscular, six-foot-four black man with only one eye probably did much to add to his image as a "dangerous nigger." Malcolm always wondered what had become of his father's other eye, but neither of his parents ever explained why the one eye was missing.

The Black Legion came to hate this "uppity Negro" who dared dream of owning his own store, and who spread unrest among "the good niggers" of East Lansing. But their hatred only fueled Earl's enthusiasm for spreading Garvey's teachings.

Malcolm's father occasionally took him along to U.N.I.A. meetings. ". . . There were never more than a few people [at these meetings]," Malcolm would write later in his autobiography. "But . . . I noticed how differently they all acted, although sometimes they were the same people who jumped and shouted in church. But in these meetings both they and my father were more intense, more intelligent . . . I can remember hearing of 'Africa for the Africans,' 'Ethiopians, awake!' And my father would talk about how it would not be much longer before Africa would be completely run by Negroes—'by black men' was the phrase he always used." Malcolm also fondly recalled the photos of Marcus Garvey, riding through Harlem in a shiny black car, dressed in an elegant uniform with gold braid, wearing a tall hat with plumes fanning in the breeze, and leading a parade of black people through the city streets. "I remember how the meetings always closed with my father saying . . . Up, you mighty race, you can accomplish what you will!"

Malcolm loved those meetings. Out of the eight children, he was the only one Earl ever took. Malcolm was never quite sure why.

One night in 1931, Malcolm and the other children woke up to the bloodcurdling screams of their mother. They rushed from their beds to find her surrounded by white policemen. The children knew at once that something was wrong with their father.

The police took Louise to the hospital to identify her husband. Earl's body was covered by a sheet. His head had been crushed on one side, and his body was cut nearly in half. He'd been found stretched across the streetcar tracks. Officially he'd died when he was run over by a streetcar. However, most Lansing blacks believed that he'd been attacked and killed by members of the white racist group the Black Legion. Those rumors were never proven to be false.

At about the same time that Malcolm lost his natural father, the man who would one day be his spiritual father was building the membership of the first temple of the Nation of Islam a few miles away, in Detroit, Michigan. That man was Elijah Muhammad. But in 1931, young Malcolm Little had never heard of him.

Earl Little was the fifth man in his family to die by violence, but he would not be the last. Years later, his brother Oscar, Malcolm's uncle, was to die from gunshots fired by northern white police. Then, later still, his seventh child was to die by an assassin's bullet. Violent death became a cruel legacy of the Little family.

Louise mourned bitterly for the loss of her husband. Friends from church and from U.N.I.A., a number coming from towns miles away, visited the Little house. They did everything they could to comfort Earl's new widow, but nothing soothed her. She was completely hysterical up to the day of the funeral.

Malcolm was six years old when his father died. He didn't remember much of the funeral, except that it was not held in a church, which he found strange. There was one other thing that stood out in his memory: Someone had put too much white powder on his father's rugged black face.

3

A Family Divided

THE WEEKS FOLLOWING Earl's death were marked by a mixture of chaos and change. Wilfred, the oldest son, quietly quit school and went looking for work to help ease his mother's financial burden. Malcolm's big sister Hilda assumed responsibility for the babies. Six-year-old Malcolm and his brother Philbert were too busy fighting with each other to be of any help to their mother.

Shortly after the funeral, Louise pulled herself together and gave her attention to the family finances. She filled out the necessary paperwork to cash in Earl's two life insurance policies. It was unusual for a black man to carry life insurance in those days but, as it turned out, Earl's extraordinary efforts to provide for his family were largely wasted. Louise had no trouble cashing in the smaller policy. However, the company holding the larger policy refused to honor it, claiming that Earl had committed suicide. Everyone in Lansing knew that the claim was utterly ridiculous, and many said as much. Nevertheless, the company stuck by its claim and Louise could do nothing to force them to pay.

The small policy helped pay for the funeral and take care of a few bills, but after that, there wasn't much left. When the insurance money finally ran out, Louise was forced to ask the local grocer for credit. This was a difficult thing for her to do. "Credit is the first step into debt and back into slavery," Malcolm's father used to say. But Malcolm's father was gone, and at thirty-four, Louise Little was left to care for her eight children alone. She did the best she could. Still, buying on credit was better than accepting Welfare. That was one thing Louise Little refused to do as long as she had breath in her. So, with Hilda home to watch the younger children, Louise went looking for work.

Traveling into Lansing, Louise was able to pick up odd jobs doing housework or sewing. She allowed prospective employers to assume that she was white and was therefore quickly hired for a variety of jobs. But once her employers discovered that she was black, and the widow of Garveyite Earl Little to boot, she was fired on the spot. The very next morning, she would go out and get another job. As before, everything was fine until Louise's new employer found out who, and what, she was. It soon became clear that she would be unable to hold a steady job.

Louise became desperate. She had to find a way to feed her babies—and fast. She realized that if her family were to survive, she was going to need help.

Malcolm came home from the Pleasant Grove School one day to find his mother talking to someone from the Welfare Board. Soon thereafter, Louise began to receive two monthly checks. One was a widow's pension. The other was a Welfare check. Louise Little thought she had finally hit rock bottom, but she was wrong.

From that point on, Welfare officers always seemed to be hanging around, dropping in without giving notice, asking Louise personal questions and quietly suggesting that she had somehow failed in her responsibility as a mother.

Young Malcolm sensed the tone of disrespect the Welfare people used when speaking to his mother. But he sensed something else as well. "They acted as if they owned us, as if we were their private property," Malcolm said later. It was as if the children suddenly belonged to the state rather than to their mother, or to each other.

Louise bitterly resented this intrusion on her family's privacy and everyone knew it—especially the children. Malcolm heard his mother speak sharply to the social workers on many occasions, pointing out that she was a grown woman, able to raise her own children without their interference or constant supervision. However, nothing Louise said or did discouraged the Welfare workers from returning month after month, for as long as the Littles were "on relief," the social workers felt they were entitled to come when they chose and say what they liked.

Malcolm didn't help matters much. He and his brother Philbert continued their fighting at home, and the two would often team up at school to fight white children. They managed to stay in trouble most of the time and the Welfare people were well aware of it.

As time went by, Louise watched painfully as the Welfare workers drove wedges between herself and her children. They would occasionally pull Malcolm or another child aside, asking him questions about his mother, using the child as a family spy. Or they would tell the children something negative about their mother, or tell one child that he was smarter, handsomer, or somehow better than his sisters and brothers. Whether each act of division was calculated, no one can say. However, the state workers did make one thing clear: They felt that Louise should allow her family to be divided so that the children could be farmed out to various foster homes. "I think they felt that getting children into foster homes was a legitimate part of their function," Malcolm wrote in his autobiography. Malcolm's mother disagreed. She was determined to keep her family together.

In 1934, during the worst of the Great Depression, the Littles were still hanging on—barely. There were days when Louise would give Malcolm and another child a nickel, and they would walk two miles to a Lansing bakery to buy sacks of day-old bread and cookies. When they got home, their mother would make French toast, or stewed tomatoes and bread, or bread pudding, and that would be their evening meal. Some days they had oatmeal or cornmeal mush, served for breakfast, lunch, and dinner. On other days, there was no food in the house at all, and the children would be dizzy with hunger. That's when Louise would go outside and pull dandelion greens and boil them up for supper. It wasn't bad enough, thought Malcolm, that kids at school teased him for being on relief. Now they teased him about eating "fried grass," too! The once-proud, self-reliant Little clan didn't have much to be proud of anymore.

Malcolm and his brother Philbert, who had finally stopped their constant fighting, did their part to put food on the family table. In the summer, Malcolm occasionally worked as a strawberry picker. At other times, he and Philbert hunted rabbits and muskrats and sold them to white neighbors. ". . . They just did it to help us," Malcolm eventually realized. ". . . They, like everyone else, shot their own rabbits." The boys never kept any for their own family to eat because their mother still had very strict dietary practices.

Malcolm started hanging around stores in Lansing after school, stealing apples or other treats. He also got into the habit of dropping in at the home of family friends, just in time for dinner. They always invited him to join them, and Malcolm would stuff himself with whatever they happened to be serving.

One of the homes he visited most often was that of Mr. and Mrs. Gohannas and their nephew, "Big Boy." Malcolm liked this older black couple and their nephew, and they were very fond of him. Still, even the Gohannases knew that Malcolm was no angel. "Malcolm," Mrs. Gohannas would say, "there's one thing I like about you. You're no good, but you don't try to hide it. You are not a hypocrite."

Malcolm didn't restrict his stealing to shops in Lansing. He and other neighborhood boys stole watermelons from nearby pastures, and sometimes Malcolm was caught. His mother tried to break him of the habit. She beat him soundly each time he was caught, but then he'd go out and steal again. Eventually the Welfare people started talking about taking him away.

A religious group called Seventh Day Adventists began to pay regular visits to the Little home. Louise responded to their teachings and soon was taking her family to their weekly meetings. Malcolm didn't think much of the religion, but the members of the congregation, which was 99 percent white, were very kind. And, more important to him at least, they always served wonderful food at the end of each meeting.

Throughout this period, the state Welfare workers continued to press for the breakup of the Little family, and Malcolm was their key. His persistent stealing gave the social workers an excuse to openly criticize his mother for failing as a parent. They were systematically building a case against Louise and she knew it. When she lashed out at them verbally, they began to say that she was crazy. It was a word Malcolm would hear time and time again. His mother refused to eat rabbit, and that was "crazy." She rejected a neighbor's offer of a pig, and that was "crazy." It didn't matter that Louse had never believed in eating pork or rabbit. As far as the state Welfare people were concerned, Louise Little was insane.

Of course, these social workers had no idea just how "crazy" Louise could get. They made the mistake of going behind her back and interviewing the Gohannases as possible foster parents for Malcolm. When Louise found out, she erupted into a volcano of white-hot rage. She shocked them into silence. Even so, when her shouting was over, the Welfare people were still pressuring Louise to turn her children over to the care of the state.

In 1935, Louise thought she'd found the solution to her problems. She began keeping company with a working man who was very stable and financially independent. He was a big black man—almost as big as Earl, in fact. Louise hoped his very presence would help in the discipline of Malcolm and his brothers, for the boys were too much for her to handle alone. With this man's help, she was sure she could pull her family together again and bring order back into their lives. And perhaps she was right, but she never had a chance to find out because, after a year, he stopped coming around. He dropped out of her life as suddenly as he had first appeared. Apparently he was not prepared to take on the responsibility of providing for eight children.

His disappearance was the beginning of the end for Louise. She descended into a state of complete despair from which she never recovered.

Malcolm continued to be a discipline problem for Louise and, eventually, the state did take Malcolm away from her. He was sent to live with the Gohannases.

Malcolm loved his brothers and sisters, and his mother, too. But he was almost relieved to be sent away. "We children watched our anchor giving way. . . . It was something terrible that you couldn't get your hands on . . . a sensing that something bad was going to happen . . ." Whatever it was, Malcolm was glad for a chance to get away from it for a while. It never once occurred to him that this separation would become permanent.

As weeks passed, Louise showed less and less interest in the house, or in the care of her children. Hilda took over more of the responsibility for the young ones and did most of the cooking. The children were uncombed and unwashed, and the house was untidy. Louise talked to herself constantly. Malcolm went home to visit frequently, but he couldn't stand to see his mother falling apart before his eyes. He was glad when the visits were over and he had to go back to the Gohannases home.

In 1937, Malcolm's mother suffered a complete nervous breakdown. She was committed to the State Mental Hospital at Kalamazoo, where she would remain for twenty-six years.

At long last, the State Welfare Board divided up the Little family. Malcolm's brother Philbert was sent to the home of a Mrs. Hackett. Reginald and Wesley went to live with a family named Williams, who were friends of Louise's. Yvonne and Robert ended up with a West Indian family named McGuire. The two oldest children, Wilfred, then seventeen years old, and Hilda, who was sixteen, were considered old enough to live on their own, and so remained in the four-room house their father had built in East Lansing.

Malcolm liked living with the Gohannases. He and Big Boy got along well, though it was not the same as being with his own brothers and sisters. "I didn't want to leave Wilfred," Malcolm wrote years later. "I looked up to and admired my big brother. I didn't want to leave Hilda, who was like my second mother. Or Philbert; even in our fighting, there was a feeling of brotherly union. Or Reginald, who was especially weak from the hernia condition he was born with, and who looked up to me as his big brother who looked out for him, as I looked up to Wilfred. And I had nothing, either, against the babies, Yvonne, Wesley, and Robert." Still, Malcolm had no choice in the matter. The state had placed him in that home and he was there to stay for a while. At least he was fortunate enough to end up with a likable companion in Big Boy.

Malcolm and Big Boy both attended Lansing West Junior High School, went fishing and hunting together in their free time, and accompanied Mr. and Mrs. Gohannas when they went to church on Sunday. They were very religious people and had once been

Baptists, like Malcolm's father. Now they went to a new church where people shouted God's praises out loud, and danced in the aisles when they felt the Spirit of God blow on them like a mighty wind.

Malcolm enjoyed his new school. Unlike Pleasant Grove School, which he'd attended earlier, West Lansing Junior High was a predominantly black school, in the center of the black community.

Malcolm was tall for his age, so it is little wonder that he was asked to play basketball. He wasn't terribly good at first, which didn't bother him, for he was more interested in trying out his boxing skills. It was 1937 and Joe Louis had just become heavyweight champion. Suddenly every black boy in America wanted to become a boxer just like Joe. Malcolm was no exception. But that was not the only reason. Malcolm's real motivation was jealousy. Philbert was gaining a reputation as a boxer in Lansing's amateur division and Reginald, who had always admired Malcolm, was now looking up to Philbert instead. Malcolm didn't like that. He decided to jump in the ring and show his little brother that he could be a good boxer, too.

Malcolm was thirteen years old when he signed up for his first fight. The minimum age was sixteen, but Malcolm was tall enough to lie about his age. Later on, he probably wished that he hadn't. He was matched with a white boy named Bill Peterson. The boy whipped him soundly. Malcolm was so humiliated that he didn't dare show his face back in the black community. ". . . In those days," said Malcolm, ". . . the ring was the only place a Negro could whip a white man and not be lynched." Consequently, a Negro who allowed himself to be beaten by a white boy was considered a disgrace. Worse yet, his little brother Reginald, who he'd tried to impress, was too embarrassed even to mention the fight.

Malcolm was determined to redeem his reputation. He went back into the gym, trained as hard as he could, and signed up for a rematch with Peterson. The fight was disastrous. A few seconds after stepping into the ring, Malcolm lay flat on the mat, listening to the referee count to ten. Fortunately his brother wasn't there to see it. "I was particularly grateful for Reginald's absence," said Malcolm. "It was probably the shortest 'fight' in history."

Having wisely given up on the idea of being a boxer, Malcolm concentrated on being the school bad boy. One day he wore a hat to school and walked into class, not bothering to remove it as he knew he should. The teacher ordered him to keep the hat on and to walk around the room until told to stop. "That way," said the teacher, "everyone can see you. Meanwhile, we'll go on with class for those who are here to learn something."

Malcolm was not about to let the teacher have the last word. On one of his tours of the classroom he placed a thumbtack on the teacher's chair. When he heard the teacher yell out in pain, Malcolm ran from the classroom, laughing. The result was predictable. He was expelled.

Malcolm was not surprised. He'd been asking for trouble. But what did surprise him was learning that the state Welfare Board had decided to remove him from the Gohannas home and to send him to reform school.

Malcolm was in shock. Being expelled for a prank

was one thing, but being sent to reform school at the age of thirteen was quite another. He was somewhat relieved, though, when told that he'd be sent to a detention home first. He solemnly packed up his things and said good-bye to the tearful Gohannases. Mr. Maynard Allen, one of the kindest Welfare workers Malcolm had met, drove him to the detention home in Mason, Michigan, twelve miles from Lansing.

Malcolm's ride to Mason seemed to take forever. At last Mr. Allen turned into the driveway of the detention home. Malcolm peeked through the car window, relieved to find that the home looked more like a dormitory than a prison. Mr. and Mrs. Swerlin, a white couple who ran the detention home, seemed nicer than he expected, too. "They were good people," Malcolm noted. "Mrs. Swerlin was bigger than her husband . . . a big, buxom, robust, laughing woman, and Mr. Swerlin was thin, with black hair and a black mustache and a red face, quiet and polite, even to me."

Malcolm's new guardians waved good-bye to Mr. Allen, then welcomed Malcolm to the home and showed him to his own room—the first he'd ever had in his life. He ate dinner with them that night and every night—also a first. He'd sat at the same table with white children before, but never with white adults. There were other children in the detention home as well, and they all sat down to meals together.

The Swerlins were very kind people. However, like most whites in Malcolm's experience, they were terribly condescending toward blacks. They frequently talked about "niggers" as though Malcolm was not even present—much the way that old slavemasters had discussed slaves while their own slaves were in the room.

The Swerlins liked Malcolm and kept him around long after he was required to move on to reform school. This was highly unusual. Most of the children at the detention home were eventually given a date in juvenile court, and then sentenced to time in a reform school. But not Malcolm. The Swerlins grew so fond of him that they sent him to Mason Junior High School and allowed him to settle in. The school was predominantly white, but Malcolm got along well there, being the token "nigger."

The Swerlins were very influential in the town of Mason and the favor shown them was extended to their new ward. They got Malcolm a job washing dishes in a local restaurant so that he could make pocket money. They also encouraged him to do his best in school, always careful to give him praise.

Of all Malcolm's classes, he liked English and history best. There was one thing, however, that he didn't like about history. His teacher always joked about "niggers." On one occasion, the teacher laughed his way through the passage on black history in the school textbook—which was only one paragraph long. Afterward, he "joked" about "niggers" having such big feet that "when they walk, they don't leave tracks, they leave a hole in the ground." Malcolm didn't find his comments very funny. Still, he did his best to pretend that these remarks didn't get to him.

While at Mason, Malcolm became serious about basketball. He made the team easily and traveled with them to neighboring towns to play. Whenever Malcolm stepped out onto the court, he heard people in the audience calling him "coon," "nigger," or "Rastus." But he, like his coach and teammates, ignored the name-calling. His teammates had used the words themselves often enough, and Malcolm had been called such names throughout his life. He was used to them, and had gotten into the habit of letting them slide off his back.

After the games, the school Malcolm's team was visiting usually gave a dance. That was when Malcolm found himself standing on the sidelines. Playing on the same team with white boys was allowed, but dancing with white girls was definitely not. Leaning against the wall of the school gymnasium and watching his teammates out on the dance floor, Malcolm found himself feeling more like the team mascot than one of its players. Rather than standing around alone the whole evening, he usually came up with an excuse to make an early exit.

Though Malcolm restrained himself from contact with white girls at school dances, his white schoolmates frequently put him up to propositioning several of the white girls around Mason. They would tell Malcolm that they had already had these girls themselves. Later, Malcolm learned that they had used him to set the girls up, figuring that a white girl who said yes to a "nigger" would surely say yes to their advances. If nothing else, they could always use the encounter as future blackmail, something to hold over a girl's head.

Malcolm actually liked a few of these girls, though he never let on. He was more drawn, though, to the black girls in Lansing his brothers Wilfred and Philbert had introduced him to. Malcolm was too shy to approach them, though he didn't understand why. He never felt that shyness with white girls.

Except for dating, Malcolm's life in Mason seemed to be on track. He did extremely well in school—his grades were among the school's highest—and in seventh grade Malcolm was elected class president, an unusual accomplishment for a black student in a white school. It was the first time he officially stepped into the role of leader, but it would not be the last. The Swerlins were proud of their black charge.

Each Saturday, Malcolm traveled to Lansing to visit his brothers and sisters. It was important for him to know how they were doing. He would also visit the Gohannases when he was there, and they were always happy to see him.

Wilfred and Hilda still lived in the four-room house their father had built. Hilda kept the house in spotless condition while Wilfred worked wherever he could.

Philbert was developing quite a reputation as an amateur boxer. Malcolm's brothers Reginald and Wesley were doing well in school and big brother Malcolm—he was fourteen—made a habit of giving them each a few of the dollars he made from his dishwashing job after school. The babies, Yvonne and Robert, were happy and healthy as well. He gave them each a quarter whenever he visited. Malcolm felt good to know that the Little children were holding their own.

Louise Little was another story. The children rarely talked about her, and they never mentioned their father. They simply didn't know what to say. Occasionally the older ones would go to Kalamazoo to visit their mother, but the visits were always disturbing. This broken woman was not the strong, proud person they'd known and loved in their younger years. She was little more than a sad stranger, clothed in their mother's skin.

During this time, Malcolm's half sister, Ella Collins, came to visit from Boston. She was a big woman, every bit as black as her father, and just as proud. It had been a long time since Malcolm had been around a black person who was proud of being dark skinned, and she made quite an impact on him. "This was the woman my father had boasted of so often. . . ." said Malcolm. ". . . She owned property . . . she was in 'society' . . ." Ella was a no-nonsense woman who spoke her mind and gave the impression that she could get whatever she wanted out of life. Malcolm had never met anyone quite like her.

Ella had countless questions about the family. She wanted to know how each child was doing. She was especially proud of Malcolm's good grades and his election as class president. Malcolm, in turn, found out a few things about his father's other children, Earl and Mary. Like Ella, they were both grown. Earl was a big-band singer in Boston, using the name Jimmy Carleton and Mary seemed happy. Ella also told him about other relatives. She'd sent several of them money so that they could leave Georgia and move north, as she had done years earlier. "Us Littles have to stick together," she said. This was the first time since leaving Lansing that Malcolm had a sense of family, of belonging.

Ella's visit was memorable for another reason. While in Lansing, she gathered the children and took them to see Louise. It was the first time all the children had gone at once, and the first time Ella and Louise had seen each other in years. Louise was happy to see Ella, and this visit turned out to be one of the most pleasant any of them had experienced.

Ella went to the home of each child before returning to Boston. She told Malcolm to write to her often and invited him to spend the summer with her in Roxbury, the section of Boston where she lived. Malcolm could hardly wait!

In the summer of 1940, Malcolm boarded a Greyhound bus for Boston. Ella was glad to see him and encouraged him to explore Roxbury. Malcolm was overwhelmed.

The size of Boston alone impressed him. Then there were the big bands, the nightlife, the throngs of blacks. He saw black-white couples walking arm in arm, and visited churches filled with black folk. He tried to write his sisters and brothers about Boston, but he found the city too hard to describe. Everything he saw was new and exciting to him. So exciting, in fact, that the summer swept by in a blur. It was soon time to return to Mason.

Back home, Malcolm suddenly found himself uncomfortable around whites. He couldn't explain what he was feeling, or why, but he felt different. Everyone around Malcolm began to sense it, too.

One day his English teacher, Mr. Ostrowski, told Malcolm it was time to think about a career. Malcolm hadn't given his future much consideration, but thought that he might like to be a lawyer. To his surprise, his teacher, a well-meaning white man, advised him against it. "Malcolm," he said, "one of life's first needs is for us to be realistic. A lawyer—that's no realistic goal for a nigger. You need to think about something you *can* be. . . . Why don't you plan on carpentry?"

Malcolm was stunned. He played the conversation over in his mind many times during the following days. He became painfully aware that, while the teacher had discouraged him from his goals, Mr. Ostrowski was quick to encourage the white students to pursue *their* stated goals. That might not have bothered Malcolm but for one thing: He was smarter than most of them. His high grades proved it.

This incident was the match that lit a new flame in the mind and heart of Malcolm Little. He began to feel something he couldn't define. It was a slow burning anger, but he didn't know it then. He only knew that he had changed inside—and there was no going back.

Malcolm began to withdraw from white people. He became, for the first time in his life, keenly sensitive to the word "nigger." Now when it was used, he would turn and stare the speaker down. His white classmates and teachers suddenly found themselves increasingly uncomfortable in his presence.

Things were no better at the Swerlin home. Everyone kept asking Malcolm what was wrong, what had changed, but he wasn't able to explain. Finally, Mrs. Swerlin decided that it was best for Malcolm to leave the detention home. It wasn't an easy decision for her. She made it with tears in her eyes. In fact, before sending him away, she tried one last time to reach him. "I guess I've asked you a hundred times, Malcolm—do you want to tell me what's wrong?" "Nothing, Mrs. Swerlin," answered Malcolm, feeling bad. He didn't know what else to say.

The Swerlins sensed his deep unhappiness and so,

in the end, sent him to live with a local black family, the Lyonses until he finished the eighth grade.

For the next two months, Malcolm concentrated on his school work, kept up his weekly visits to Lansing to see his brothers and sisters, and wrote to Ella in Boston. Sending Ella a letter almost every other day, Malcolm let his half sister know that he wanted to come live with her in Boston.

Ella responded to his pleas. She gained custody of Malcolm and had his files transferred from Michigan to Massachusetts. As soon as Malcolm completed the eighth grade, he packed his bags and headed for the bus station. He was on his way to Boston, and to a whole new life.

4

From Hick to Hustler

BOSTON WAS THE most spectacular world Malcolm had ever known. It had crooked cobblestone streets with tall buildings pressed so tightly together he was sure they were holding each other up. He saw fast and finely polished Cadillacs cutting through busy traffic. There were fancy hotels and restaurants in the white part of town, and subway trains that sped through underground tunnels. Malcolm took his first ride on one, getting off near the campus of Harvard University. He toured the campus, fingering the architecture of its great halls, never guessing that in twenty years he would be invited to speak in one of those very buildings.

Of course this was not the first time he'd been to Boston, but he hadn't seen much of the city during his previous brief stay with Ella. Now, at Ella's suggestion, Malcolm explored every inch of it. After each day of discovery, Malcolm returned to Roxbury or the "Hill" as it was called, where professional and property-owning blacks like Ella lived. There he would sit down to a platter piled with the kind of soul food his Georgia-born father had loved, and his mother had hated: ham hocks, collard greens, black-eyed peas, grits and gravy, fried fish and cabbage, and a huge helping of sweet potatoes. Malcolm couldn't get enough of it.

He couldn't get enough of Boston, either. He gawked at the air-conditioned cinemas downtown, deciding that he would see every movie that came to town. He wandered through old Boston, marveling at the historic sites, markers, and statues of famous men. Here he learned of the black man Crispus Attucks, the first man to fall in the Boston Massacre. The place that Malcolm spent most of his time in, though—to Ella's great dismay—was the black ghetto.

Malcolm was most comfortable in the ghetto, among working-class blacks who felt free to be themselves—unlike the more "sophisticated" Hill blacks with whom his half sister wanted him to spend time. Malcolm hated the way they imitated the speech, mannerisms, and haughty airs of whites. Their houses were nice enough, but Malcolm preferred the ghetto's grocery stores and storefront churches, walk-up flats and wild parties, pawnshops and poolrooms. It was in one of those poolrooms that Malcolm met a man named Shorty, his first friend in Boston.

Shorty was a stubby young man ten times darker and ten years older than Malcolm though Shorty never knew it. He worked in a poolroom racking up balls for the players. Malcolm had often stared at him and the other "cool cats" through the poolroom window. Shorty had come out once and spoken to him, leading Malcolm to think of Shorty as a friendly sort.

Malcolm had been in town for a month when he decided he needed to get a job. Ella offered to find one for him, but Malcolm decided to surprise her by finding one on his own. That's what led him to walk into the poolroom one day to ask Shorty to help him find a job racking up balls. "I don't know of no pool joints around here needing anybody," said Shorty. Then he asked Malcolm what kind of work he'd done in the past. When Malcolm mentioned working as a dishwasher in Mason, Shorty's face lit up. "My homeboy!" he shouted. "Man, gimme some skin! I'm from Lansing!"

Now Malcolm knew he'd come to the right place. Where else in Boston was he likely to meet someone from his own hometown? Not on the Hill, that much he knew for sure.

Malcolm was excited to discover that he and Shorty knew many of the same Lansing black families. He and Shorty became fast friends, and Shorty took Malcolm under his wing to teach him the way things worked in the big, bad city of Boston.

First, Malcolm had to learn the language. There were words like "cat," "chick," "cool," "hip," "Daddy-o," "jive," and "groovy," and expressions like "frantic scene," "juke-down mellow," and "dig the action." Even work was referred to in a strange way. A job was called a "slave," and working was "slaving." Malcolm wondered if he'd ever memorize this new vocabulary.

Next, Shorty helped him find a "slave" as a shoeshine boy at a place called the Roseland State Ballroom in a part of Boston called Back Bay. Malcolm was astonished by what he saw.

If Roseland wasn't heaven, Malcolm was sure the pearly gates were just around the corner. All the great big bands played there: Glenn Miller, Benny Goodman, Duke Ellington, Count Basie—every famous band of the 1930s and '40s performed at the Roseland State Ballroom. They played sweet, sad songs called the blues, and foot-stomping dance songs with names like "Redskin Rhumba." But no matter what they played under those soft, rose-colored lights, Malcolm loved it.

Malcolm turned away from the ballroom and climbed up to the second floor looking for Shorty's friend, Freddie. Freddie was the shoe-shine boy Malcolm would be replacing. He had come into a lot of money and no longer needed the job. He was glad to turn it over to Shorty's "homeboy," and to help Malcolm learn the ropes.

Freddie taught Malcolm the best way to organize his supplies, and how to shine a shoe until it glistened. He told him to keep an eye on the men's room and to run up and offer a hand towel to each man before he exited. He could earn a few extra pennies that way. He told Malcolm where the shoelaces were and how much to charge for them. Then he told him to keep a couple dozen packs of condoms in supply in case a customer needed to buy a pack after a dance.

Freddie told Malcolm that there were other ways to make extra money at this job. He called those ways "hustling." A hustle was a legal, or illegal, way to make money without going to work at a regular nine-to-five job—money that you didn't have to pay taxes on. Selling goods at twice their original price would be a legal hustle, while selling drugs would be an illegal hustle. Anyone who did this kind of work was called a hustler, and besides being a shoe-shine boy, that's exactly what Freddie was.

"Some hustles you're too new for," explained Freddie. "Cats will ask you for liquor, some will want reefers." Malcolm knew all about reefers. Shorty had taught him how to smoke them to get high. "But you don't need to have nothing except rubbers—until you can dig who's a cop," Freddie continued. "The main thing you got to remember is that everything in the world is a hustle." Malcolm listened carefully.

Once Malcolm had the language down and had settled into his new job, Shorty got to work on his young friend's appearance. First he sent Malcolm to a neighborhood clothing store to be fitted for a zoot suit in a color of his choice. Malcolm chose sky blue. The pants were thirty inches wide at the knee and tapered down to twelve inches at the hem. The matching coat pinched the waist and flared out below the knees. This was the hottest style among hip young blacks in the forties, and Malcolm had wanted such a suit ever since he'd first seen one. Besides the suit, Malcolm chose a wide-brimmed blue hat with a feather, a gold-plated chain that swung below the coat hem, and a narrow leather belt with the initial *L* on it for Little.

Malcolm hadn't been working long enough to be able to afford this new getup, but Shorty only shook his head and laughed. "Homeboy, you never heard of credit?" asked Shorty. Malcolm had, of course. It was just that he'd always been taught to save for what he wanted. However, Shorty convinced him that buying on credit was something everyone did. So, for the first time in his life, Malcolm signed a credit agreement. He picked out exactly what he wanted and walked out of the store without paying a dime. "I was sold forever on credit," Malcolm said years later.

Finally, Shortly invited Malcolm to his apartment so that Shorty could give Malcolm his first "conk." A conk was a processed hairstyle that most black "cats" wore in those days because, while nobody said so, having hair "like whitey" was considered the coolest.

Of course a person really had to want a conk badly to get one, because the chemical used for removing the natural curl from a black person's hair was lye, and it burned terribly.

Shorty gave Malcolm a list of things to buy in preparation: Red Devil lye, two eggs, two potatoes, Vaseline, soap, two combs, a rubber hose, a rubber apron, and a pair of gloves. When Malcolm brought him everything, Shorty mixed the lye, potatoes, and eggs and got started. He massaged Malcolm's scalp with Vaseline, and applied thick layers of Vaseline to his head and neck. Malcolm didn't know why until Shorty combed the lye mixture through his hair. At first, Malcolm felt a little warmth and nothing more. But moments later, his red hair felt like a flaming torch that burned through his scalp and sent fingers of pain shooting from the back of his head to his brow.

Malcolm gritted his teeth while his eyes watered and his nose ran. When he couldn't stand the pain anymore, he darted for the washbasin. Shorty rinsed the lye out and washed Malcolm's hair several times.

Shorty combed and shaped the limp hair, rubbing more Vaseline into it. He used a razor to shape the hair in the back and to create sideburns. Then he handed Malcolm a mirror.

Malcolm was thrilled. His shining red hair was thick and smooth, and as curl free as any white man's.

Young Malcolm was certainly a long way from Lansing now. He'd forgotten those early lessons about self-reliance, credit-free living, dietary restrictions, and race pride. Reverend Earl Little, the Garveyite, could scarcely have recognized the person this son of his had become.

Malcolm was a fast learner. It didn't take him long to figure out that the biggest part of the job of shoe-shine boy at the Roseland was hustling reefers and liquor and slipping the telephone numbers of black prostitutes to white "johns", or customers. Most of the dances were for whites only, and it was common for white men to come around at the end of the dances looking for "black chicks." If they offered Malcolm a tip, their wish was his command. Now Malcolm was a hustler, too.

Occasionally, when things were quiet enough on the second floor, or when Malcolm could find someone to watch his stand for a few minutes, he'd go down to the ballroom to listen to the big-band sounds and watch the couples glide across the dance floor. He'd never seen such glamorous white women in his life. He never thought about dancing with them, though, because Malcolm didn't dance.

Malcolm frequently hung out with Shorty after work, shooting dice, playing cards, or dropping in on parties at somebody's "pad." At one of these parties, a girl pulled Malcolm out onto the dance floor before he could stop her. For a moment, he stood rooted to the floor in the middle of the jostling crowd. Then, half high on alcohol or marijuana—or both—he let his African instincts take over and, to his surprise, he started dancing.

That first dance was purely improvised, but in the weeks to follow, Malcolm learned to do the lindy-hop, the most popular dance of the day. "From then on," said Malcolm, "hardly a party took place without me turning up—inviting myself, if I had to—and lindy-hopping my head off."

Malcolm could hardly keep his feet still at the shoe-shine stand. He felt like dancing all the time now. The next time he learned that a blacks-only dance had been scheduled, with Lionel Hampton's band playing, Malcolm gave up his shoe-shine stand so that he could be there to dance beneath the rose-colored lights.

Ella was pleased with the news. She hadn't wanted Malcolm to take that job in the first place. She was concerned about the company her fifteen-year-old brother was keeping. As soon as she knew he'd given up the shoe-shine job, she asked around the neighborhood until she found Malcolm a job she considered suitable.

There was an opening for a soda-fountain clerk in a drugstore two blocks away, and as far as Ella was concerned, the job was perfect. Malcolm would have a chance to mix with "some of the nice young people" who lived on the Hill. Malcolm detested those Hill types, with their air of superiority, but Ella had been kind to him, and he didn't want to anger her. He took the job without argument.

Weeks of making ice cream sodas for those phonies, wearing a dull, uncomfortable white jacket, was almost more than Malcolm could take. He couldn't wait to get home at night to change into his zoot suit and go out lindy-hopping or getting high with his friends for relief. But even looking forward to those wild nights was not enough after a while. He was just about ready to quit his job when a girl named Laura started coming in.

Laura was a small, brown-skinned girl who arrived

every afternoon for a banana split. Malcolm noticed that she was different from the other Hill girls. She was natural and friendly, though she always sat by herself and read a book while she ate her banana split. Looking at her with her head stuck in a book on algebra or Latin, Malcolm realized he hadn't read so much as a newspaper since he'd left Mason. It would be a long time before he started reading again, though.

After four or five weeks, Malcolm started striking up conversations with Laura. They talked about high school, her love of learning, their respective backgrounds. Malcolm mentioned his long-forgotten interest in becoming a lawyer, which he immediately wished he hadn't. Laura jumped on the subject and refused to let it rest. "Malcolm," she would say, "there's no reason you can't pick up right where you are and become a lawyer." Of course, the truth is, Laura had no idea "where" Malcolm was—as a hustler, reefer smoker and peddler.

One afternoon, Laura mentioned that she loved lindy-hopping. Malcolm was delighted to learn that they had that in common and wasted no time inviting her to a dance at the Roseland. Count Basie would be playing.

Laura's eyes popped with excitement, but she explained that she lived with a strict and very religious grandmother who did not approve of dancing. Laura knew that she would never be allowed to go.

"Maybe some other time," said Malcolm, letting the subject drop.

The day before the dance, Laura stopped by the drugstore with a surprise. She'd changed her mind about the dance, and she was going. For the first time in her life, she'd lied to her grandmother, saying there was something going on at school the night of the dance. She asked Malcolm if he'd still take her. Malcolm agreed, but first she had to stop by the house with him after work so that he could change.

When Malcolm walked through the door with Laura, Ella could not have been more pleased. She'd been after Malcolm to meet a nice young girl from the Hill, and Laura fit the bill. By the time Malcolm went up to his room, changed clothes, and came back down, Laura and Ella were acting like old friends. Malcolm was sure Ella was already planning the wedding he and Laura would have.

Laura didn't quite know what to make of Malcolm in his wild zoot suit, but once the two were out on the dance floor at the Roseland, lost in the music and the lindy-hop, she knew that they made a wonderful pair.

Malcolm took her home early that night so she wouldn't get in trouble with her grandmother. Malcolm thought that dance would be a one-time thing for her, but Laura was hooked. The next time she heard about a blacks-only dance, she asked him to take her. This time, though, she told him to pick her up at home. She refused to hide her love of dancing from her grandmother anymore. Malcolm hesitated, but finally agreed.

As soon as he neared Laura's house, he could feel the tension. Her grandmother took one look at him and his zoot suit and glared at him with angry eyes. Those eyes spoke plainly: she blamed him for corrupting her innocent young granddaughter.

While he waited for Laura, neither he nor Laura's grandmother spoke. By the time Laura appeared, coat in hand, the tension was unbearable. They left quickly and grabbed a taxi. Almost immediately, Laura burst into tears.

Between sobs, Malcolm learned that Laura and her grandmother had had an awful fight, a screaming match in fact. Laura had told her grandmother that, in the future, she would be going out to dance or to do anything else she pleased, and her grandmother would just have to learn to accept it.

When the taxi pulled up in front of the Roseland, Laura wiped her eyes and put the fight behind her. She and Malcolm joined the throng moving out onto the dance floor and, in no time, were caught up in the music.

Toward the end of each blacks-only dance, the band-leader called for "showtime." That's when everyone left the floor except the very best dancers. The women would take off their heels and slip on white sneakers. Then the dancing would really begin and each couple in the spotlight would try to out-dance the others. At that second dance, Laura and Malcolm were one of the couples on the floor.

"Go, Red, go!" the crowd yelled. Everybody at Rose-land called Malcolm "Red." He was one of their favor-ites. Laura was about to become one, too. She had a unique style of lindy-hopping, with moves as smooth as a ballet dancer. Her style made quite a statement and, when she and Malcolm danced together, every-body stopped and stared.

One of the people staring at them was a beautiful white woman named Bea. It wasn't unusual for white women to come to the all-black dances hoping to meet some "black studs." But Malcolm had never seen one as beautiful and sophisticated as Bea. She caught his eye, and he caught hers. When the dance with Laura ended, he and Bea moved out to the dance floor together. At that moment, Malcolm forgot about Laura completely.

Malcolm took Laura home early, then returned to the Roseland to meet Bea. She invited him out for a drive in her convertible and they slipped off to a deserted spot on the outskirts of Boston. It was the first of many nights they would share.

Malcolm never took Laura out again. In fact, she never returned to the drugstore soda fountain the rest of the time he worked there. It hurt her to see the sparks going off between Malcolm and Bea, and all she wanted to do was get out of the way.

As for Malcolm, he was too busy showing off his new white lady to think much about Laura. It was a big status symbol for a black man to have a white woman like that at his side, and he knew it. Not only was she blond and beautiful, but she had money as well—and she didn't mind spending it on Malcolm.

Malcolm's stature in black Roxbury grew overnight. He was suddenly noticed by club managers, known gamblers, and a variety of major league hustlers. He had less and less time for Shorty, but Shorty didn't seem to mind. Actually, Shorty was proud of him. "Man," he'd say, grinning, "I had to comb the burrs out of my homeboy's head, and now he's got a Beacon Hill chick."

Malcolm's "chick" took good care of him. When Shorty began sleeping over at the home of a woman he was seeing, Bea gave Malcolm the money to move into half of the apartment. Shorty stayed in the apartment once in a while, but otherwise Malcolm had the place all to himself. It was just as well, because Ella made it clear that she had no use for Malcolm once he dropped that "sweet girl" Laura and started dating Bea.

About the time that Malcolm moved from Ella's house, he quit working at the drugstore and took a job as a busboy at the Parker House restaurant in downtown Boston.

A few weeks later, he came into work and found the kitchen crew in shock. The Japanese had just bombed Pearl Harbor.

World War II brought with it a variety of employment opportunities for black men. Many jobs held by whites who were suddenly drafted needed to be quickly filled. Some of those jobs were with the railroad.

Ella heard about such a job from one of her friends. It was on the New Haven Railroad. She suggested it to Malcolm, hoping to get him out of town—and away from Bea. Malcolm had no intention of giving up Bea, but he liked the idea of free travel. He'd been hearing fantastic things about New York City from as far back as he could remember, and knew that working for the railroad was one sure way to see "The Big Apple" for himself. He needed to be twenty-one years old to get the job. He was only sixteen so he lied about his age. It was hardly the first time.

Malcolm began his new job by loading shipments of food onto trains in the Dover Street train yard. Later, he was temporarily assigned to work as a dishwasher on The Colonial, a train that ran from Boston to Washington, D.C.

The kitchen crew worked in tight quarters while waiters shouted out the customers' orders over the noise of clacking train wheels, whistling engines, clanging pots and pans, and the clatter of silverware against plates and saucers. Malcolm had never seen as many dirty dishes and greasy pots and pans as he did on that five-hundred mile journey to the capital. But the hard work was worth it. When the train pulled into Washington for an overnight layover, Malcolm had a chance to explore the nation's capital for the first time in his life.

Malcolm was thrilled to see the White House, the Washington Monument, and the Lincoln Memorial. But he was shocked at the number of dirt-poor blacks living in shacks along lanes called Pig Alley and Goat Alley. These were filthy ghettos filled with bums, drug dealers, prostitutes, crap-shooters, and small children running around in the middle of the night barefoot and begging for money. What surprised Malcolm most was that these ghettos were only a stone's throw from the White House and the monuments celebrating the equality of men.

There were blacks in Washington who lived better than the residents of Pig Alley, of course. They were Howard University graduates who worked as cab drivers, porters, bank guards, janitors, and so on. The most distinguished position a black person with a college degree could hope for in those days was that of a mail carrier for the U.S. Post Office.

Malcolm stayed on the Colonial for a few more weeks until a temporary opening came up on the Yankee Clipper train which ran from Boston to New York City. Malcolm packed his zoot suit and was ready to go.

That first visit to New York was one he'd never forget. The cooks from the Yankee Clipper grabbed a cab up to Harlem and took Malcolm with them. Downtown New York passed by in a blur of bright lights, fancy restaurants, impossibly tall buildings that spiraled into the night sky, and everywhere, white faces. But once the cab got above 110th Street and Central Park West, the faces that stared back at Malcolm were the tan and copper and coffee-colored faces of black folk. This was Harlem, U.S.A.

Malcolm's first stop was a place on Seventh Avenue called Small's Paradise. The Yankee Clipper crew had told him it was their favorite night spot in Harlem. As soon as Malcolm walked through the doors, he understood why.

Unlike the loud and rowdy ghetto bars Malcolm was familiar with, Small's had a hushed atmosphere where conservatively dressed men spoke in quiet tones and slowly sipped their drinks. The large circular bar had comfortably cushioned seats around it, and the people seated there had an air of genuine sophistication quite different from the phony mannerisms of the Boston Hill blacks Malcolm so detested. These men were well-known gamblers and gangsters with a history of connections to the Mafia.

From Small's, Malcolm headed for 125th Street to see the world-famous Apollo Theatre. From there he could see the Theresa Hotel, the only luxury hotel in New York City where blacks could stay. It was also the hotel Fidel Castro chose to stay in when he visited the United Nations.

One block away was the Braddock Hotel, whose bar was a famous hangout for black celebrities. It was there that Malcolm saw such stars as Billy Eckstein, Ella Fitzgerald, Billie Holiday, and Dinah Washington.

Malcolm heard that Dinah and Lionel Hampton were both appearing at a place called the Savoy Ballroom. He made that his next stop.

The two-hundred-square-foot dance floor of the Savoy Ballroom made Malcolm drop his jaw. The Roseland couldn't begin to compare with the Savoy's size or grandeur. Where the Roseland had one bandstand, the Savoy had two. It also had a revolving stage in the rear. Many of the booths against the wall were filled with whites who'd come as much to watch the blacks dance as to listen to the big-band music.

From the Savoy, Malcolm wandered along Lenox, Seventh, and Eighth avenues, staring wide-eyed at the clusters of black soldiers and sailors passing by, the pimps and hustlers that darted in and out of dark hallways, offering prostitutes and peddling "hot" rings and watches that might have been stolen that very day.

By the time Malcolm climbed aboard the Yankee Clipper to return to Boston, he knew he hadn't just visited a different city. He had been to a different world. It was a world that he would soon make his home.

For the time being, though, Malcolm busied himself selling sandwiches, coffee, candy, cake, and ice cream to passengers on the Boston–New York run. He made a grand show of serving them, pretending to be an "Uncle Tom," a black person who was ready and willing to bow and scrape and do anything to please a white person. His performance was always worth an extra sale or two, and in no time Malcolm was earning more money for the railroad than the man he had temporarily replaced. By the time the original sandwich man was available for work, the railroad had reassigned him and given his job to Malcolm permanently.

Now Malcolm was able to explore Harlem on a regular basis. He took a room at the Harlem YMCA for a while so that he'd have a place to stay during layovers.

Malcolm loved New York City in general and Harlem in particular. He ventured into every part of it, from Sugar Hill, where many famous stars lived, to the darkest, dirtiest slums. He took in the pawnshops and dope peddlers, the cursing cab drivers and sleek Cadillacs that hogged far too much parking space. He slipped into sleazy bars and past numerous storefront churches that had *Zion* somewhere in their names, as so many black churches did. He saw the alcoholics and addicts huddled on the street corners. He sniffed salt pork, collards, chitterlings and fried chicken cooked in various soul-food restaurants throughout Harlem. He saw dozens of barbershops that specialized in giving conks and as many beauty shops where black women could get their hair pressed and curled and could catch up on local gossip. Malcolm took in every detail of the city's mean streets. In the end, he could actually feel the energy of the city flow up through the soles of his feet.

Malcolm became a regular at Small's Paradise and the bar of the Braddock Hotel. He met and befriended musicians such as Duke Ellington's drummer, Sonny Greer, and violinist Ray Nance. The bartenders at Small's knew him so well they started pouring his favorite brand of bourbon as soon as they saw him walk in the door.

Malcolm began to pick up the speech and roughness of the Harlem street hustlers, and his behavior on the

Yankee Clipper began to change. He cursed constantly and openly showed disdain for the white servicemen who rode the line. The kitchen crew took bets on how long he would last.

Even when Malcolm wasn't intentionally causing problems, trouble seemed to find him. Once a very large and very drunk red-faced soldier from the south blocked his path and said, "I'm going to fight you, nigger." Using his quick wit, Malcolm laughed and said, "Sure, I'll fight, but you've got too many clothes on." Layer after layer, Malcolm kept the soldier stripping until he was bare from the waist up. Each of the passengers was laughing by then, and the man's fellow soldiers led him away out of embarrassment. "I never would forget that," Malcolm later wrote, "I couldn't have whipped that white man as badly with a club as I had with my mind."

Malcolm may have talked his way out of that situation, but he wasn't able to stay out of trouble for long. The railroad received passenger complaints about him continually so it came as no surprise to anyone when he was finally fired. Malcolm didn't mind, though. He took the money the railroad owed him and made a trip to Lansing to visit his brothers and sisters.

His oldest brother Wilfred was away in Ohio, studying a trade at Wilberforce University. But Philbert and Hilda were still working in Lansing. Reginald was planning to sign on as a merchant marine. Yvonne, Wesley, and Robert, the youngest, were all in school.

No one in Lansing was prepared for the likes of Malcolm. They hardly recognized this wild young man with the flaming-red conked hair, bizarre zoot suit, and vulgar vocabulary. But Malcolm thought he was cool, so while everyone in Lansing was laughing at him, he was laughing at them. He didn't feel much like laughing, though, when he visited his mother in the state hospital at Kalamazoo. She only had a vague sense of who Malcolm was.

While he was in Lansing, Malcolm paid a special visit to Shorty's mother and let her know that her son was healthy and had money in his pockets. She gave Malcolm greetings to pass on to her son, and thanked Malcolm for stopping by.

Lastly, he traveled to Mason to see Mrs. Swerlin. He'd changed a lot since his days in the detention home that she and her husband ran. Everything about the way Malcolm looked and sounded shocked her, and Malcolm quickly realized that his presence was making her uncomfortable. He found it best to make a hasty exit.

Back in New York, Malcolm signed up with the railroad's Seaboard line and got a job renting pillows to passengers between New York and Miami. But that job was short-lived because he and the conductor, a "redneck" from Florida, hated each other.

As it happened, Malcolm wasn't out of work for long. That same afternoon, when he dropped into Small's Paradise for a drink, the bartender told him that one of their waiters was going into the army. The job was open, if Malcolm wanted it.

Malcolm thought he had died and gone to heaven. There was no place he'd rather be than Small's Paradise. It was in the very heart of Harlem, and Malcolm had long been ready to make Harlem his home.

There were a few sacred rules anyone who worked at Small's Paradise had to accept: no lateness, no laziness, no stealing, and no hustling of customers—

especially men in uniform. Malcolm happily accepted every one. In fact, he found the first rule especially easy to follow. He was so excited about working at Small's that he usually showed up an hour early.

His boss, Charlie Small, liked his attitude. So did the morning waiter who worked the earlier shift. He gave Malcolm tips on getting along with the cooks and bartenders, and on pleasing the customers.

The waiter wasn't the only one who offered Malcolm free advice, either. Cooks, bartenders, and customers often pulled him aside to teach him how to identify plainclothes policemen, and how to tell major league hustlers from small-time operators. They gave him the background on men with names like Black Sammy and King Padmore, Cadillac Drake and Jumpsteady. And customers who were expert hustlers themselves taught Malcolm the inner workings of their own particular hustles. These men were well liked and highly respected.

It was at Small's that Malcolm learned the history of Harlem and developed a mental catalog of local cops and criminals. One of the most feared hustlers was West Indian Archie, a man who had once worked for gangster Dutch Schultz. Men such as Archie were known to have "persuaded" people with lead pipes, wet cement, baseball bats, and brass knuckles.

Millions of blacks in urban areas spent money every week "playing the numbers," just as they do today. Playing the numbers meant placing a bet on a three-digit number and hoping to match the last three figures of the stock exchange's daily total of domestic and foreign sales. With odds of six-hundred to one, the winning number could make someone rich overnight. The people who accepted the bets and who paid off the winners were called numbers runners. A few runners like "the West Indian" were known for accepting only large bets.

Small's was not strictly a hangout for hustlers, though. There were lots of ordinary nine-to-fivers who dropped in for drinks after work. And Small's was one of the few night spots recommended to whites who traveled uptown for entertainment. But it was the criminal element that Malcolm found most attractive, for he admired men who could live by their wits.

Soon after starting work at Small's, Malcolm moved into a rooming house in the 800 block of St. Nicholas Avenue. The building was full of petty thieves and hustlers, dope peddlers and prostitutes. Many of the prostitutes befriended him, treating him like their little brother. They saw the teenager behind the mask of maturity that he wore.

Bea came from Boston to visit Malcolm fairly frequently. Malcolm introduced her to everyone at Small's and quickly discovered that even in New York, among the most sophisticated blacks, being with a white, blond beauty gave him special status. "We would go to the Braddock Hotel bar," wrote Malcolm, "where we would meet . . . musicians who now would greet me like an old friend. 'Hey, Red—who have we got here?' They would make a big deal over her." Malcolm knew, of course, that the fascination blacks had for whites was the same as the fascination whites had for blacks. When the downtown nightclubs and the regular Harlem bars closed for the night, the Harlem after-hours bars and speakeasies had white people from wall to wall. "These whites were just mad for black 'atmosphere,' " wrote Malcolm.

One such speakeasy was run by Creole Bill, a man

from New Orleans. The speakeasy was actually his apartment. He kept soft music on the record player, offered a variety of drinks, and sold plates of spicy Creole gumbo and jambalaya which he made himself.

One night when Malcolm and Bea were at Creole Bill's, a white man who Malcolm knew came over to talk to them. The man was a "hippie," a young white who tried his best to look, sound, and act like a hip black man. Malcolm introduced Bea, then left her long enough to greet a good friend. When he returned, Bea told him that the man had asked her why she was wasting herself on a black man. "This was my best early lesson in how most white men's hearts and guts turn over inside of them . . . whenever they see a Negro man on close terms with a white woman," wrote Malcolm.

Soon thereafter, Malcolm learned that Bea had married a wealthy enlisted white man while he was on leave from the army. This was a marriage of financial convenience, however, and did not affect her relationship with Malcolm. She continued to see him as before.

Malcolm had been in Harlem for a while now, and it was time for him to be given a nickname. People had always called Malcolm "Red," but there were two other well-known Reds in Harlem already. St. Louis Red, a burglar, was one, and the other was a comic called "Chicago Red." He and Malcolm eventually became good friends and remained so even after the world came to know Chicago Red as the comedian Redd Foxx.

Just as the two other Reds were named for cities, so was Malcolm. When people asked him where he came from, he'd say Detroit, Michigan, because few New

Yorkers had ever heard of Lansing. Consequently he came to be known as "Detroit Red."

Malcolm's work at Small's Paradise ran smoothly from spring 1942 until early 1943. Then one afternoon, Malcolm broke one of the club's cardinal rules: he hustled a customer, and a man in uniform at that.

It started out innocently enough. Malcolm saw a lonely-looking black soldier drinking at one of his tables and asked the man if he wanted a woman. (Malcolm lived, remember, in a building full of prostitutes, many of whom were his personal friends. It was easy enough for him to give the man one of their telephone numbers—and that's just what he did.) But almost immediately, Malcolm sensed that he'd made a big mistake. He was right. The "soldier" turned out to be one of the military spies the army sent to Harlem night spots to flush out hustlers who were guilty of "impairing the morals" of servicemen.

Malcolm told Charlie Small what he'd done and was immediately fired, as he'd expected. It saddened Charlie to let Malcolm go, but he had to protect the reputation of his club. Malcolm understood.

Malcolm was taken to a local police station but was not booked. Fortunately, Malcolm had refused to take money in exchange for the prostitute's phone number. He'd never been in trouble with the police, either, and that was in his favor. Still, he didn't walk away scott-free, for he had been barred from Small's Paradise, and for Malcolm, that was the worst kind of punishment.

Malcolm wasn't sure what to do next, but Sammy the Pimp, who he'd met at Small's, offered to help him get started in a hustle of his own. The question was, Which one?

The choice turned out to be simple. They both knew merchant marines who could bring good marijuana into the country easily, and Malcolm knew enough musicians who smoked to have a ready-made market. Consequently, peddling reefers seemed like the natural hustle for him.

Sammy gave Malcolm twenty dollars to buy his first batch of marijuana. Later that evening, Malcolm returned the twenty and had plenty left over. In no time, he was making fifty to sixty dollars a day, clear profit. ". . . This was a fortune to a seventeen-year-old Negro," said Malcolm. "I felt, for the first time in my life . . . *free*. Suddenly, now, I was the peer of the other young hustlers I had admired."

During the daytime Malcolm frequently went to the movies, sometimes seeing five shows in one day. At other times, he'd hop a train for Boston to see Bea and to visit Ella for a while. Malcolm appreciated the help Ella had given him, and he liked to give her a little money now and then as a way of saying thanks.

While in Boston, he visited his old friend Shorty, and he and Bea went out to hear Shorty's new band. Shorty had somehow managed to get a 4-F classification from the military, which meant that he was unfit for duty, and did not have to join the army and go off to war.

Back in Harlem, Malcolm's business was quite successful until police started keeping an eye on him. He began carrying small packages of reefer under his armpit so that he could duck into a doorway or around a corner and quickly drop the evidence if he thought he was being followed. That didn't keep police from trying to catch him, though. One night, when he came home, he saw that someone had been in his room and had gone through his belongings. Malcolm moved out immediately and found another rooming house. After that, he made a point of changing residences from time to time, just to be safe.

It was during this period that Malcolm graduated to carrying guns. His first was a .25 automatic. Malcolm's hustle was becoming complicated. He spent so much time and effort staying one step ahead of the narcotics squad that his sales dropped. He couldn't sell as openly to his wealthy musician friends as he once had, but was instead forced to sell to street-corner addicts who didn't mind the complicated hide-and-seek arrangements he had to make to protect himself. Still, Malcolm felt the police closing in. Then Sammy gave him an idea.

"Red, you still got your old railroad identification?" he asked. Malcolm realized that he had. "Well, why don't you use it to make a few runs until the heat cools?"

Malcolm didn't know why he hadn't thought of it before. If the musicians couldn't come to him in New York, he could check their tour schedules and use the railroad to go to them. Like most inventive ideas, it was really quite simple. Overnight, Malcolm became "the traveling reefer peddler."

Returning to New York from one of these reefer runs one afternoon, Malcolm found his little brother Reginald waiting for him. The merchant ship that Reginald worked on had docked in New York harbor for repairs.

Malcolm was glad to see his little brother. Of course, Reginald wasn't so little anymore. He was sixteen years old and six feet tall.

The two brothers talked into the night. Malcolm told

Reginald things about their father that Reginald hadn't remembered, and Reginald told Malcolm the latest on his other brothers and sisters.

Malcolm took his favorite brother around to the hot Harlem night spots and showed him off to everyone. He knew that Reginald's ship was in port for only a week, and wished that his brother could stay longer. It was only natural, then, that he encouraged Reginald to leave the merchant marine and come live and work with him in New York. "I'll think about it," promised Reginald. Malcolm smiled, impressed that his little brother hadn't just jumped at the chance. He saw in Reginald a degree of maturity he admired.

The brothers said good-bye and promised to stay in touch. Meanwhile, Malcolm had a more immediate concern. Uncle Sam had caught up with him. He was to be drafted into the army.

"In those days only three things in the world scared me," wrote Malcolm. ". . . Jail, a job and the Army." Malcolm knew he had to come up with a fool-proof way to beat the draft, and he had less than two weeks in which to do it.

First, knowing that army intelligence had spies in various hangouts around town, Malcolm started talking about how anxious he was to join the army—the *Japanese* Army. He made sure to talk loudly enough for anyone interested to hear. Then he rummaged through his clothes to find the perfect costume for his draft board appointment.

Finally, the critical day arrived. Malcolm carefully frizzed his hair until it stuck out all over, then dressed in a loud-colored zoot suit. Ready for his appointment, he went downtown to the draft board office and skipped in the door talking a mile a minute, and using the loudest, hippest street language he knew.

When he was called into the office of the army psychiatrist, Malcolm kept looking over his shoulder as though he were convinced that someone was behind him, listening in on his private conversation. Then, without warning, he leapt up from his chair, peeked under the doors, and whispered into the psychiatrist's ear. ". . . I want to get sent down south. Organize them nigger soldiers, ya dig? Steal us some guns and kill up crackers!"

Malcolm's performance was brilliant. The psychiatrist dropped his pencil and fumbled around for another while he tried to find his voice. When he did, he quickly dismissed Malcolm and asked the receptionist to send in the next man.

Shortly thereafter, Malcolm received a 4-F classification card in the mail saying that he was "mentally disqualified for military service." He refolded his zoot suit and packed it away. He wouldn't be needing it anymore.

Malcolm worked a variety of hustles over the next two years. He ran numbers and sold bootleg whiskey to after-hours bars and speakeasies. He never became a full-fledged pimp, but he did work as a "steerer" for a white madam, secretly transporting wealthy whites to special houses of prostitution in Harlem. Together with his friend, Sammy the Pimp, Malcolm carried out small stick-up jobs and armed robberies as well.

He and Sammy came close to getting caught twice, and once Sammy was grazed by a guard's bullet. That was the last time he joined Malcolm in a robbery attempt.

"I was a true hustler," Malcolm wrote in his auto-biography. ". . . Uneducated, unskilled at anything honorable, and I considered myself nervy and cunning enough to live by my wit, exploiting any prey that presented itself."

Part of Malcolm's nerve came from the five guns he now owned, the opium he smoked, and the cocaine he sniffed on a daily basis.

High or sober, Malcolm's various hustles kept the money flowing, and he started placing his numbers bets with West Indian Archie.

One of the things that made the West Indian so special was his photographic memory. He could look at hundreds of number slips during the course of a day and file every number in his head. He never had to carry betting slips. Consequently, if he were stopped and searched by the police, they would never find any evidence of illegal activity. This made him the safest numbers runner in Harlem and explained why people like Malcolm, who spent one hundred dollars or more per week playing numbers, put their trust—and their money—in the West Indian's hands.

While Malcolm was busy betting with Archie, his brother Reginald left the merchant marine and came to New York to stay with his big brother. Malcolm took an apartment—the first he'd ever rented on his own—to provide a sense of "home" for his brother. It was located on 147th Street between Convent and St. Nicholas avenues, roughly the same area he had roomed in for years.

Malcolm set Reginald up with a safe, legal hustle. He taught Reginald to buy cheap items from down-town manufacturers, and then sell them as "hot" or stolen items at twice the price to people in barbershops, beauty salons, and local bars. It was a great hustle, and Reginald was good at it. However, he gave it up after a short while, having found an older woman who was willing to take care of him.

Meanwhile, Malcolm continued to live on the edge, leaning dangerously over a deep, dark pit, never noticing how close he was to falling in. He was too busy running hustles, doing dope, and listening to the music of Billie Holiday.

It was 1945. Malcolm was twenty years old.

5

Prison Bound

MALCOLM'S HEART BEAT wildly as he stepped from a cab at 147th Street and St. Nicholas, in front of La Marr-Cheri, one of his favorite clubs. His mind was in a fog of fear and cocaine as he and a friend, Jean Parks, entered the bar. They had a few drinks together and then he sent her home alone. Between the cocaine and the bourbon, he was too high to travel.

He had a .32 stuck in his belt, pressing against his rib cage, but it wasn't much company or comfort because Malcolm was more frightened than he had ever been. West Indian Archie was after him and Malcolm knew that Archie might kill him before the night was over. Malcolm was glad that Reginald was out of town because his baby brother might have tried to protect him, and that could have meant more trouble for them both.

Earlier that day, Malcolm had collected three hundred dollars from Archie for a number he had hit. According to Archie's famous photographic memory, Malcolm hadn't placed a bet on that number. He paid

Malcolm anyway, though. He figured that if Malcolm had actually hit the number, he would get that three hundred dollars back when he collected for that day's betting. However, when Archie checked the betting slips later, he found that he was right. Malcolm hadn't bet on the winning number after all. Either Malcolm had made a mistake, or Malcolm was trying to cheat him. Archie couldn't take the chance that he was being cheated. That would be bad for his reputation on the street.

Malcolm had to worry about his reputation, too. As frightened as he was of Archie, he had to stand up to him in public, or he'd lose respect among all the other hustlers in Harlem. Pretty soon, other hustlers would be trying to push him around, and he'd have to spend so much time looking over his shoulder that he'd have no time left for hustling. He couldn't afford to let that happen. That's why he sat on a barstool in La Marr-Cheri in plain sight, knowing that West Indian Archie might come in at any moment.

The bar suddenly grew silent. In the hush, Malcolm looked up into the barrel of the gun West Indian Archie pointed at him. Malcolm thought about reaching for the pistol stuck in his belt, but Archie read his mind.

"You're thinking you're going to kill me first, Red. But I'm going to give you something to think about. I'm sixty. I'm an old man. I've been to Sing Sing [prison]. My life is over. You're a young man. Kill me, you're lost anyway. All you can do is go to prison."

Neither man moved. Fortunately for Malcolm, Archie let two of his friends pull him to the rear of the bar. Malcolm took his time before leaving. He stood out front for five minutes so that no one could say he had run from Archie. When Archie failed to follow him, Malcolm left.

For the next two days, Malcolm stayed high on marijuana, Benzedrine, and opium. It was the only way he knew to fight back his fear.

Everywhere Malcolm went, people avoided him, for word had spread through Harlem that West Indian Archie was out to kill him, and nobody wanted to get in Archie's way.

The tension got to Malcolm. He was ready to reach for his gun at the slightest hint of trouble. Two nights after his encounter with Archie, a young hustler started an argument with Malcolm in a bar. Malcolm punched him in the mouth, and the boy—he was just a teenager—pulled out a knife. Someone grabbed the boy and threw him out of the bar before Malcolm could shoot him. Humiliated, the boy loudly threatened to kill Malcolm the next time he saw him.

Malcolm returned to his barstool. He felt the pistol still safely tucked in his belt. He'd come close to using it on that boy, and that would have been a mistake. He knew he had to stay in control of his emotions or he was lost.

Intuition told Malcolm to get rid of his gun, and he did. Just moments after slipping the gun to another hustler in the bar, a policeman came through the door. The policeman knew that Archie was after Malcolm and was sure Malcolm was armed. Malcolm followed the policeman outside and the officer's partner searched for a gun.

"Red, there's a report you're carrying a gun," said the first officer.

"I had one," said Malcolm. "But I threw it in the river."

The officer gave him a warning. "I think I'd leave town if I were you, Red."

Sammy the Pimp must have been thinking the same thing the day before. That's when he had placed a call to Boston and told Malcolm's friend Shorty that he'd better come and take Red back to Boston for a while. But Malcolm had no idea that Sammy had placed such a call.

Having left the bar, Malcolm walked down St. Nicholas Avenue, nervously studying the darkness for any sudden movement. He heard a car horn beep behind him and froze.

"Homeboy!" called Shorty. Malcolm spun around, ready to draw his gun. When he saw his old friend, he relaxed.

"Daddy-o!" said Malcolm. He climbed into Shorty's car. Shorty drove Malcolm to his apartment, explaining about Sammy's phone call on the way. At the apartment, Shorty stood guard outside while Malcolm packed the few things he wanted to keep. Shorty helped him load his things in the trunk of the car and the two took off for Boston.

Shorty hadn't slept for thirty-six hours, but he had no trouble staying awake. Malcolm talked nonstop during the entire drive.

Boston hadn't changed much since Malcolm had left, but Malcolm had. Shorty realized that when he had his old friend move back in with him. Malcolm had turned into an atheist who cursed constantly, began each day by getting high off reefers, and was suspicious of everyone—Shorty included.

Malcolm's first month back in Boston passed quietly. He spent two weeks catching up on his sleep, then went into the streets to find a local cocaine supplier. Once he had cocaine in his system again he felt "normal".

He went to see his half sister Ella, who was sad to see how her promising young brother was turning out.

Bea came to see Malcolm several nights a week. Her husband was out of the military, but his new job as a salesman kept him away from home as much as the army had. That made it easy for Bea to continue her relationship with Malcolm without her husband finding out.

Bea usually came to the apartment when Shorty was out performing with his band, but when Shorty came in later, Malcolm would mention that she'd been there. Simply knowing that Bea had been there made Shorty glad, because he loved having white women around.

Shorty's love of white women was no secret to Bea. Perhaps that's why she brought her seventeen-year-old sister, Joyce, with her to Shorty's apartment on one of these visits. Shorty and Joyce liked each other immediately. Shorty liked Joyce because she was white and young, and she was fascinated with Shorty because he was black and a musician. Joyce and Shorty decided they were a perfect match.

After four weeks in Boston, Malcolm began to get restless. He needed to find a new hustle, but first he needed a stake—a large amount of money that he could invest in a new scheme. If he was going to sell drugs, he'd need money to buy a large supply to get him going. If he was going to become a big-time gambler, he needed to get into games that required a minimum bet of five hundred or a thousand dollars. No matter what the hustle, Malcolm would need a lot of money to start out with.

Bea gave Malcolm money when he asked for it, as she always had. It was never enough money to start a new hustle with, but Malcolm knew that he could multiply the amount by playing a few good hands of poker. All he had to do was find a gambling house. He found one owned by a gambler named John Hughes.

Hughes was considered an excellent gambler, but he soon discovered that he was no match for Detroit Red. Malcolm beat him and three other gamblers out of five hundred dollars in a single game. Afterward, John told the man who managed his gambling house, "Any time Red comes in here and wants anything, let him have it."

The respect John Hughes showed Malcolm was reported throughout the Roxbury underworld, and Malcolm's reputation as a cool-headed gambler was set. From that night on, he moved comfortably among the best-known gamblers and hustlers in Roxbury.

Malcolm was respected—and feared—for another reason as well. When anyone played cards at John Hughes's gambling house, he was asked to leave his guns at the door. Malcolm went along with that, always handing over two guns. But one night, another gambler tried to cheat him during the game and Malcolm pulled a third gun from a shoulder holster. People called him crazy and trigger-happy after that, but they left him alone.

It didn't take Malcolm long to build up a small stake. Once he had, he decided on a hustle: house burglary. The stake gave him enough money for all the burglary tools he would need, as well as cash for a getaway car and a base of operations.

Malcolm chose burglary rather than gambling because he wanted a hustle that could include Shorty. Shorty was always broke and Malcolm felt sorry for him. He knew Shorty could make more money hustling then he ever could by working a regular job or performing with his band.

Shorty surprised Malcolm. Not only did he happily agree to go along with Malcolm's robbery scheme, but he also suggested that Malcolm invite a young man named Rudy to join them.

Rudy was a waiter for private parties in several of the most exclusive areas of Boston. It would be easy for him to choose a good house for burglarizing, and to find out where the owners kept their valuables. When Malcolm told Rudy he was forming a burglary ring, Rudy said, "When do we start?"

Malcolm was in no hurry. He had learned from expert burglars in New York that careful planning was the key to success. Malcolm took his time so that he could consider every angle. He had to decide what kind of houses to rob, what time of day to carry out the robberies, how to get rid of the stolen merchandise, what kind of tools were needed, and so on. He had a lot to think about.

Malcolm knew that Rudy could tip them off to some nice houses, but not to all of them. There were homes in wealthy white sections of Boston that only whites could get into. Malcolm was certain that Bea could get herself invited to such homes. It would be easy for her to find out where the jewels and other valuables were kept and to discover whether or not the house had an alarm or security system. He was also certain that she'd agree to do it if he asked her, and he was right. Bea joined the burglary ring and talked her sister into participating as well.

Once the burglary ring was formed, Malcolm looked around for a "fence," someone who would buy the stolen property and give him cash. He found one sooner than he expected. He never actually met the fence himself, but he met the man's representative.

The arrangements were simple: Malcolm would contact the representative before a robbery and tell him what the gang expected to steal. The rep would give Malcolm the address of a warehouse where they could unload the stolen items. The fence would decide how much the goods were worth. Then, in two or three days, the rep would meet Malcolm and give him the cash.

Last but not least, Malcolm had Bea and her sister rent an apartment in Harvard Square to use as a base of operations. They could make their plans from there and use the apartment as a meeting place late at night without being noticed.

The gang began meeting at the apartment to make final plans. They decided that Bea and Joyce would find the best houses to rob. They'd go in pretending to be saleswomen or poll takers and take a good look around. Later they'd draw the layout of the house for Malcolm, showing where the valuables were. Two of the men would carry out the robbery and the third would stay in the getaway car, with the motor running, and keep watch.

A working plan was set. All that remained was for the gang to choose a leader. Malcolm chose himself. He knew exactly how to get everyone else to agree.

Malcolm pulled a gun out in front of the gang and emptied the five bullets out onto a bed. He put one bullet back in and spun the chamber around, then held the gun up to his head. "Now I'm going to see how much guts you all have," he said, and pulled the trigger. They all heard the gun click. Everyone begged Malcolm to stop, but he pulled the trigger a second time. Again they heard a click. The second cylinder was empty like the first. But was the bullet in the next cylinder? Malcolm pulled the trigger again.

Bea and her sister were hysterical. Even Shorty and Rudy were terrified. But Malcolm had made his point. Slowly he lowered the gun. "I am not afraid to die," said Malcolm. "Never cross a man not afraid to die." The fear and awe Malcolm saw in everyone's eyes told him that no one in the gang would dare to question his leadership, and no one ever did.

Malcolm and his gang robbed their first house later that night with great success. A few robberies later, they had their routine perfected: they used passkeys and lock picks; they'd enter through windows or from the roof; they'd steal whether people were away or asleep in their beds. They stole watches, wallets, handbags, jewelry, and clothes. Sometimes they'd take a tip from their fence and steal specialty items. During one period, for instance, they stole Oriental rugs. A small one would bring as much as a thousand dollars.

These robberies were usually problem free, but the gang did have a few close calls with police. It was Malcolm's quick thinking that saved them. Once when they were making their getaway, a police car patrolling the area followed them to find out what blacks were doing in a wealthy white section of town. Malcolm had Rudy stop the getaway car. He jumped out and waved down the police to ask for directions. He said that he and his friends were lost and were trying to get to Roxbury. Malcolm looked so confused that the officer believed him. He pointed Malcolm in the right direction and drove away.

Between robberies, the gang would meet to party, smoke marijuana, and listen to music. Malcolm got high on cocaine, too. He used some of the money he made from the robberies to support his twenty-dollar-a-week habit, and to buy the four packs of cigarettes he went through every twenty-four hours.

Before each robbery, Malcolm stopped by a club known as the Savoy in order to establish an alibi. He had Bea call him at a phone booth there just minutes before the crime was planned. That way, people at the club could confirm that they'd seen Malcolm in the club at the time the robbery took place.

Detective Turner, a black policeman, had been keeping his eye on Malcolm since his return to Boston. The detective frequently threatened to arrest Malcolm, hoping to frighten him. But Malcolm didn't like being threatened and he let Turner know it. The two men hated each other. Turner was at the Savoy one night when the telephone rang for Malcolm. Turner stepped into the booth before Malcolm could get there. He picked up the phone and spoke into the receiver, but Bea said nothing. When she heard a stranger's voice, she hung up.

"Wasn't that call for me?" Malcolm asked the detective. Turner said that it was. "Well, why didn't you say so?" asked Malcolm. Then he and Turner exchanged sharp words.

"You know, Turner," said Malcolm, "you're trying to make history. Don't you know that if you play with me, you certainly will go down in history because you've got to kill me?" Malcolm meant what he said and Turner knew it. The detective backed down.

Malcolm's reputation for being fearless, cool, and crazy was once again confirmed.

He might have been reckless less often if he had been sober. Most of the time he was high on cocaine or reefer or both. As a result, he sometimes acted first, thought second, then suffered the consequences.

Late one evening, he stopped by a favorite night spot and saw Bea and her sister Joyce with an unfamiliar white man. The bartenders and waiters pretended not to know Bea and Joyce, which made it clear to Malcolm that they didn't want this man to know they'd been in that part of town before. But Malcolm didn't care. He waltzed up to their table and greeted them like old friends, calling Bea "Baby." Bea and Joyce turned pale.

The man turned out to be a friend of Bea's husband.

Malcolm left the club hours later and went to the Harvard Square apartment to relax. He climbed into his pajamas and was crawling into bed when he heard a knock at the door. He slid under the bed to hide. He knew something was wrong, because no one in the gang ever knocked. When he failed to answer the door, someone used a key and entered. Footsteps approached the bedroom. Someone bent down and looked under the bed. It was Bea's husband's friend.

The gentleman had dropped Bea and her sister off at home, and had somehow gotten the apartment key from one of them. Now here Malcolm and the man were, face to face.

Malcolm tried to laugh off the situation and climbed out from under the bed. The man could tell from the women's clothes in the closet that Joyce and Bea spent time there, so Malcolm didn't try to hide their relationship.

Malcolm was relieved when the man finally left, but knew that Bea's husband would probably get a call in a few days telling him that his wife had committed the one sin that could not be forgiven: She'd been having a relationship with a "nigger."

Two days later, on January 12, 1946, Malcolm went to a jewelry shop to pick up a watch he'd left to be repaired. It was a watch stolen during one of his robberies. The person who owned it had described it to the police and told them about the kind of repair it needed. Police had alerted local jewelers to be on the lookout for this watch. Consequently, when Malcolm went to pick it up, the police were there waiting for him.

Another black man entered the store and, for a moment, the policeman turned his attention to that man, thinking he was part of Malcolm's gang. Malcolm thought about pulling his gun on the policemen, but an inner voice stopped him. Years later, Malcolm would say that it was the voice of Allah.

Malcolm raised his arm and motioned to the policeman. "Here, take my gun," said Malcolm. Shocked, the officer took the gun, then called to two other policemen hidden in the back of the store. They'd been there all along. Malcolm realized that, had he drawn the gun, they would have killed him.

Malcolm was arrested quietly and taken to police headquarters. Police found his home address from the telephone book and other personal papers he had on him. Soon Shorty, Bea, and Joyce were arrested. Only Rudy managed to avoid arrest. He got out of town somehow, and was never captured.

Malcolm later learned that Bea's husband had gone to the Harvard Square apartment with a gun, looking for him. The only reason the man hadn't found and killed him is that Malcolm was in that jewelry store, a few miles away, being arrested.

Malcolm's trial came and went quickly. He and Shorty were convicted of several counts of larceny, breaking and entering, and carrying firearms without a permit and sentenced to ten years in jail. Bea and her sister received one to five years, and were sent to the Women's Reformatory at Framingham, Massachusetts.

The average sentence for first-time offenders charged with the gang's crimes was two years. Malcolm and Shorty's sentences were longer, Malcolm believed, because everyone in the justice system wanted to punish them for being involved with, and corrupting the morals of, two high-class white women. (Even Malcolm's lawyer seemed to think so. He told Malcolm that he had no business with white girls).

Malcolm and Shorty were sent to Charlestown State Prison on February 27, 1946.

Malcolm had not yet turned twenty-one.

Malcolm's prison cell was like all the others. It was cramped and filthy with a covered pail that served as a toilet. He could stand in the middle of the cell or lie on his uncomfortable cot and easily touch both walls.

Malcolm's older brother Philbert was the first to write to him in prison. He wrote that the church he attended would be keeping Malcolm in its prayers. Malcolm wrote back a nasty letter telling Philbert not to bother.

Malcolm's first visitor in prison was Ella. Unfortunately, her visit didn't meet with much more success than Philbert's letter. Neither Malcolm nor Ella knew what to say to each other anymore.

Malcolm was in a particularly foul mood those first weeks because he was going through drug withdrawal. It took a while before he learned how the prison drug-traffic system worked. When he did, the first thing he got high on was nutmeg, which he sniffed like cocaine. He learned from a cellmate that he could use cash or cigarettes to buy matchboxes of nutmeg from inmates assigned to the prison kitchen. Later he took money Ella sent him and bought marijuana and pep pills from the prison guards who sold them.

Malcolm was a troublemaker from the first day. He cursed the guards, threw things out of his cell, held up the line in the dining hall, dropped his food tray on purpose—anything that would get him sent to solitary confinement. He preferred the dark loneliness of the cells in solitary to his own cell. In solitary, he would pace back and forth, cursing the guards, God, and the Bible. His reputation was so bad that he earned the nickname "Satan."

Then Malcolm met a fellow inmate named Bimbi in 1947. Bimbi was the first black man Malcolm had ever met who was respected for his mind and his ability to communicate. Bimbi challenged Malcolm to use his brain, suggesting that Malcolm take advantage of the prison courses offered by mail. He encouraged Malcolm to borrow books from the prison library and to make good use of the time, rather than wasting it cursing at everyone day after day. Malcolm respected Bimbi and decided to take his advice.

First he signed up for a course in English. It had been one of his favorite subjects when he'd been in school in Mason. Now he could hardly write a postcard that was readable. In addition to English, he started borrowing books from the library as Bimbi had suggested.

After a year, when Malcolm felt confident that he could write a decent letter, he decided to continue his self-education, and considered what his next course should be. Bimbi had given him a new respect for language, and a curiosity about the origin of words. To satisfy that curiosity, Malcolm signed up for a course in Latin.

Those two courses by mail and the books that Malcolm read in his tiny cell gave him an appetite for knowledge and learning that would stay with him for the rest of his life.

Malcolm owed Bimbi a great debt. He would one day pay that debt in the only way that mattered: by making the most of his mind, and encouraging others to do the same.

On January 10, 1947, Malcolm and Bimbi saw each other for the last time. Malcolm was transferred to Concord Reformatory for fifteen months. It was to be the most critical fifteen months of his young life.

6

Malcolm Comes to Muhammad

MALCOLM SAT IN his cell in Concord Prison, reading the newest letter from his brother Philbert, and groaned. Philbert wrote about a new group he had joined called the Nation of Islam and urged Malcolm to "pray to Allah for deliverance." Malcolm tossed the letter aside in disgust. He thought his brother Philbert was pitiful. He had joined so many different religious groups over the years that Malcolm had no respect for his brother's sincerity. Malcolm sent Philbert a bitter reply.

Days later, Malcolm received a letter from Reginald which he read with much more interest. Reginald told him to stop eating pork and smoking cigarettes. "I'll show you how to get out of prison," wrote Reginald. Malcolm didn't know what pork and cigarettes had to do with gaining his freedom, but if giving them up could lead to his getting back on the streets, he was ready to try it.

The first time Malcolm refused to eat pork, it was big news throughout the prison. The white guards and inmates especially commented on it. Since many black people cooked with ham and salt pork and ate pigs feet, whites couldn't imagine that a black man could live without having pork in his diet. Malcolm enjoyed proving them wrong.

Malcolm wasn't the only one in his family who'd stopped eating pork and smoking cigarettes. His brothers and sisters in Detroit and Chicago had, too. They had all become members of the Nation of Islam, the same group Philbert had written him about. It was Elijah who taught them that pork and tobacco polluted the body, and should be avoided. That was the real reason Malcolm's brother Reginald had told him to give up those things. Reginald was leading Malcolm to accept Elijah's teachings one step at a time, as Malcolm would later learn.

Malcolm's half sister Ella continued to play an active role in Malcolm's life. Since his arrest, she'd learned about a pioneering prison program in Norfolk, Massachusetts, that might be able to help Malcolm change the direction of his life. The jail was called Norfolk Prison Colony, and Ella worked hard to get him transferred there. In late 1948, she succeeded.

Norfolk Prison Colony was unlike any jail Malcolm had ever heard of. The colony was an enclosed campus of twenty-four three-story house units, holding fifty inmates apiece. This was a prison without bars, where each inmate had his own room, with flushing toilets. Visitors were allowed daily, and could remain for up to two hours. What made Norfolk Prison Colony most unique, though, was its educational programs, and the general interest in learning that the inmates there all seemed to have. Where prisoners at both Concord and Charlestown were forever fighting and cursing and trading cash for drugs and cigarettes, inmates at Norfolk passed the time in group discussions, debates, and in attending classes taught by instructors from nearby Boston University and Harvard.

Best of all, Malcolm discovered, was Norfolk's library. A millionaire named Parkhurst had left his private library collection to Norfolk when he died. That collection amounted to thousands of books, many of them original editions that were no longer in print. Malcolm, like every other prisoner, was free to visit the library on his own, something he could not do at Charlestown or Concord. He spent many hours roaming the aisles of the library, fingering the spines of the books on the shelves, and selecting a few to take back to his room. "Much of the big private collection was still in crates and boxes in the back of the library," wrote Malcolm. "Any college library would have been lucky to get that collection."

Malcolm settled in at Norfolk, wondering when he might see or hear from his brother Reginald again. He was pleased when Reginald wrote from Detroit, where he now lived, saying that he was on his way to Norfolk for a visit. Malcolm remembered that Reginald had promised to show him a way out of prison. Malcolm hoped that his brother was finally going to explain his escape plan, whatever that might be.

Reginald did have something to explain to his older brother, but it had nothing to do with breaking out of prison. Reginald was interested in freeing Malcolm's mind—not his body.

"Malcolm, if a man knew every imaginable thing that there is to know, who would he be?" Reginald asked. Malcolm knew his brother was leading up to something. Reginald often took a roundabout way to make a point. But in the end, what he had to say was always worth hearing. Malcolm decided to wait patiently. "Well, he would have to be some kind of god—" said Malcolm.

"There's a *man* who knows everything . . . God is a man," said Reginald. Reginald explained that black people, God's children, were gods themselves. Among these god-men, said Reginald, was one who was the God of Gods, the Most High, the Supreme Being. "His real name is Allah."

Philbert had mentioned Allah in a letter when Malcolm was still at Concord. Reginald went on. "The devil is also a man," he said. "The white man is the devil."

Malcolm was astonished. He felt closer to Reginald than to anyone else in the world, and he'd never once heard his brother talk about God or the devil or anything else that had to do with religion. But Malcolm respected Reginald enough to hear him out.

Reginald told him that Allah was the God of the black man, that he had revealed himself to a man named Elijah Muhammad, and that Elijah offered the black man in North America "the true knowledge." Reginald shared many new ideas with Malcolm during that visit, and on each visit thereafter. Reginald talked about slavery, the history of whites oppressing America's blacks, about Malcolm's need to understand his identity as a man with roots in Africa, and more. Malcolm listened, trying to digest it all.

A black God for the black man. The idea surprised and excited Malcolm. He suddenly realized that it wasn't God or religion that he'd been rejecting all his life, but it was the *white man's* God, and the *white man's* religion—Christianity—that he'd found offensive. And why shouldn't he? Although the God of the

Bible considered all races equal and worthy of love and respect, the Christianity practiced in America supported slavery, had members that participated in racist organizations like the KKK, and generally excused the inhumane treatment of black people. Islam, on the other hand, honored the black man as a human being. That appealed to Malcolm.

Malcolm began receiving two letters a day from his family in Detroit. Philbert, Hilda, Wilfred and his first wife, Bertha, had all become Muslims. Each wrote to Malcolm about the one they called "The Lamb," the "Honorable Elijah Muhammad," and about his teachings concerning the "Lost-found Nation of Islam." And each, in his own way, urged Malcolm to accept these teachings and to bow his knee to Allah.

According to Elijah Muhammad, the "true knowledge" was this: The original or first man on the earth was black, and his home was in Africa. This black man had built mighty empires on the continent of Africa while whites were still living in the caves of Europe. The white man eventually left those caves and traveled on foot, horseback, and ships to other parts of the world. When he came across societies of non-white people, the white man raped, murdered, and oppressed them. He did this throughout history.

The white man's travels took him to Africa, where he kidnapped millions of black people and shipped them to the West Indies, to South America and North America as slaves. These blacks were forbidden to speak their own languages, live with their own tribes, play their own music, or even practice their own religions. As a result, the black man eventually forgot where he came from, and what his true identity was.

The schoolbooks, written by whites, never mentioned any of this history. Now, through the teachings of the Honorable Elijah Muhammad, this knowledge was once again available to the black people of North America.

Malcolm was overwhelmed by all these new ideas. He lost his appetite and stopped eating. Prison officials worried that he was trying to starve himself, but he was simply so intent on digesting this new information that he couldn't even begin to think about food.

Malcolm's sister Hilda traveled to the Massachusetts prison for a visit with her baby brother and gave him even more to think about. She told him a strange tale that Elijah Muhammad called "Yacub's History."

Yacub was a brilliant black scientist who lived in Mecca sixty-six hundred years ago when all the people on earth were black. Yacub was a member of the tribe of Shabazz, the tribe from which—according to Elijah Muhammad—the American black was descended.

Yacub was a born troublemaker and a bully, and was very proud of his intelligence, partly because he had figured out a way to create new races of people by breeding them like horses. His scientific discoveries made him popular—and dangerous. Allah finally banished Yacub and his 59,999 followers to the island of Patmos so that Yacub could not stir up any more trouble among the people of Mecca.

Angry with Allah, Yacub decided to create a devil white race as revenge. First he made a law that any new black babies that were born should be destroyed. Only brown babies were allowed to live. When they grew up and married each other, their babies would be brown. After two hundred years, all the people of Patmos were brown.

Now, when these brown people married, every third baby born would be red. This time, the red babies were kept alive, and all the brown ones were killed. After another two centuries, all the people of Patmos were red. This process continued for eight hundred years. The races went from black, to brown, to red, to yellow, and finally, to white. This "bleached" race of people, being lighter and weaker than Original Man, was more likely to do evil than their black brothers. That was exactly how Yacub had wanted them to turn out. He had not lived long enough to see it for himself, but the devil white race he had dreamed up in his scientific lab had become a reality.

This race remained on Patmos for another six hundred years. Then they returned to the mainland among blacks, and that's when the real trouble on earth began.

Within six months, this devil race had told so many lies and caused so much fighting among blacks that the black people put them all in chains and marched them off to the caves of Europe. Later, Allah sent Moses to civilize them so they could re-join the world.

This devil race was to rule the earth for six thousand years.

According to "Yacub's History," all of these things had been foretold. And it was also foretold that God would appear on the earth in modern times to teach Islam, "Yacub's History," and the true knowledge to the black people in North America. That God was Master W. D. Fard. He was half black and half white so that he could move easily within the worlds of both blacks and whites in America.

In 1930, Fard met Elijah Muhammad in Detroit, Michigan, and gave him the message of Allah to pass on to the black man—the lost tribe of Shabazz—so that the black man could regain his true identity and reclaim his rulership of the earth.

This was "Yacub's History." It was no real history at all, but it did have bits and pieces of truth woven throughout. It was those bits and pieces that Malcolm responded to (though in later years, he would reject "Yacub's History" altogether).

Hilda finished telling Malcolm about Yacub and said good-bye. Malcolm was too stunned to open his mouth. The mix of fact and fantasy, the exciting intellectual environment at Norfolk, his recently renewed interest in the world of language and literature, this radically new spiritual teaching called Islam—all these combined to give Malcolm a powerful "high." Only this time, his high had nothing to do with reefers or cocaine.

Malcolm began writing letters to Elijah Muhammad. He had a difficult time writing that first letter. His vocabulary was limited and his penmanship poor. He determined then to work on improving both so that he could write better letters in the future.

Not long after sending that first letter, Malcolm got a response. Elijah congratulated Malcolm on receiving "the true knowledge" and told him that, as a prisoner, Malcolm was a symbol of white society's criminal oppression of the black man. He sent Malcolm a few dollars as well and told him to have courage. Malcolm came to the end of the letter and felt a pleasant shudder. It was signed "Elijah Muhammad, Messenger of Allah."

Now Malcolm wrote to his brothers and sisters or to Elijah every other day. His family urged him to accept Islam and, mentally, he was receptive. The idea of submission to Allah was much more difficult. For years Malcolm had laughed at black men who believed in the white man's God. But here was a God who, according to Elijah Muhammad, was black like Malcolm; a God with dark skin and kinky hair, a God to whom a black man could relate. This new black God and new religion, said Malcolm's brothers and sisters, offered Malcolm a chance to be a better person, and to live a better life than he ever had before.

Day after day, as Malcolm read the letters and pamphlets his family sent him, he began to look back on his life with new eyes. For years he had abused the body that Allah had given him by drinking and using drugs, and that was wrong. He'd used the wit that Allah had blessed him with to con and rob and steal from his people, created in the black God's own image, and that was wrong. He'd traded the bodies of black women to the devil white man for profit, and that was wrong. For the first time, feelings of guilt washed over him until he thought that he would drown. As Malcolm felt himself sinking, he cried out to Allah in prayer.

Malcolm gave his heart to Allah in that prison cell and immediately felt as though he'd come home to himself. He praised Allah for that feeling, and was grateful to the Honorable Elijah Muhammad, whose teachings had led him to Islam.

Malcolm's new faith so excited him that he wanted to share it with someone—anyone. He wrote letters to some of his old hustler friends in Boston and Harlem, but none of them wrote back. Malcolm was sure they thought he had lost his mind.

Frustrated that he couldn't express himself on paper the way he wanted to, Malcolm finally took steps to expand his vocabulary. He found a dictionary and copied the first page, word by word, as neatly and clearly as he could. It took him a day, and he spent hours reading it back to himself aloud, but the work was worth it. When he woke the next morning, he discovered that he could remember nearly every word on that page. Malcolm was proud and excited. He flipped through the dictionary, amazed at the number of words printed there. He'd never realized that there were so many words in all the world.

Malcolm went on to copy the second page, and the third, and the fourth, until he'd copied the entire dictionary. With each page, his vocabulary increased and his penmanship improved. Best of all, with his new treasury of words, Malcolm was ready to explore the thousands of books in the Parkhurst collection, confident that he'd be able to understand all that he read. Up until then, he'd always skipped over the words he didn't understand, and gone on to the next word.

Malcolm became a hermit. He disappeared into the library for hours at a time. When he wasn't in the library, he could be found in his room, gobbling up books the way a starving man gobbles up food. After lights-out at 10 P.M., he'd sit on the floor to read from the light in the hallway. Every now and then a guard would walk through to check that everyone was in bed, and Malcolm would jump into bed and fake sleep until the guard left. Then he'd return to his place on the floor and read until 3 A.M.

Elijah's teaching on "the true knowledge" made Malcolm particularly interested in history and religion, and those were the areas he concentrated on most. He read about the African slave trade, American slavery and abolition, which was the movement to end slavery. He read about Mahatma Gandhi, the Indian revolutionary who used nonviolence to get the British to give up their occupation of India. He read about the white man sending the drug opium into China, which led to many Chinese people becoming drug addicts in the early 1800s.

Malcolm also read books by great philosophers like Socrates, Nietzsche, and Kant. He was surprised to learn that one of the most famous philosophers, Spinoza, was a black Jew from Spain.

Perhaps the most important subject Malcolm read about was ancient Africa. He learned about the great kingdoms of Mali and Ghana, and the empires of Ethiopia and Egypt. And everything Malcolm read proved that the teachings of Elijah Muhammad were true.

At last Malcolm understood for himself how much he had to be proud of as a black man. Now he understood why his father had been so proud. The teachings of Marcus Garvey, the U.N.I.A. meetings he'd gone to with his father, the talk among Garvey's followers about a "glorious age in Africa"—it all came back to Malcolm.

As Malcolm's pride grew, so did his love for his black brothers. He began spending more time with the other black inmates at Norfolk. He wanted, more than anything, to talk about Islam, Elijah Muhammad, and "the true knowledge" that was transforming his life. Whenever he had the chance, he would share these ideas with his black brothers. And, if the brother seemed ready to accept, Malcolm would invite him to follow Elijah Muhammad and to join the Nation of Islam.

Malcolm discussed all the new developments in his life with Reginald when his brother came to visit. Malcolm was indebted to Reginald for introducing him to Islam. That's why Malcolm was stunned when Reginald began saying bad things about Elijah Muhammad. Malcolm was even more shocked when he learned that Reginald had been expelled from the Nation for having sex outside of marriage. Such behavior was not allowed in the Nation of Islam (N.O.I.).

Reginald's brothers and sisters urged him to beg for Allah's forgiveness and to apologize to Elijah Muhammad, but Reginald refused. He called Elijah a hypocrite. Malcolm didn't understand why at the time, but he would one day.

Malcolm was torn between his love for his brother and his new devotion to Elijah Muhammad who, he believed, had saved his life. Distressed, Malcolm wrote to Elijah defending his brother, and pleading with Elijah to forgive him. But when Elijah wrote back that Reginald's own weakness and lack of discipline had caused him to fall, and that Reginald alone was responsible for being expelled—not Elijah—Malcolm accepted it.

Malcolm and all of the other Muslims in the family turned their backs on Reginald. He was allowed to visit them and they would listen to what he had to say, but they made it clear that they were on Elijah's side, and not Reginald's. This broke Reginald's heart. He eventually ended up in a mental institution, just as his mother had years before.

Malcolm's last year in prison was spent at Charlestown. All of his talk about "the devil white man" had led authorities at Norfolk to transfer him before he could influence too many other black inmates.

Malcolm missed the freedom he had enjoyed at Norfolk. But most of all, he missed the weekly debates. He loved to use his new vocabulary to talk about African history and to show, by pointing out examples from the past, that the white man had proved himself to be the devil time and time again.

Malcolm looked for opportunities to debate topics that allowed him to discuss the evils of the white man. Since there were no debating teams at Charlestown, Malcolm attended Bible class, which many blacks attended. He longed for a chance to say something about African history or white oppression that would make those brothers stop and think about who they were, and Bible class was just the place to do it.

During one such class, the Harvard Seminary student that led the discussion was talking about the Apostle Paul. Malcolm raised his hand and asked what color Paul was. "He had to be black . . ." said Malcolm. ". . . because he was a Hebrew . . . and the original Hebrews were black . . . weren't they?" The seminary student answered honestly. "Yes." Then Malcolm went on. "What color was Jesus . . . he was Hebrew too . . . wasn't he?"

Every person in that room, whether black or white, held his breath. The instructor walked around the room, weighing his answer.

"Jesus was brown," he said finally. Malcolm smiled. He knew the story of that class discussion would be echoing off the walls of that prison for days to come.

Black inmates began looking to Malcolm with new respect. He used their admiration to great advantage, taking every chance to recruit followers for Elijah Muhammad and converts for the Nation of Islam. It was a pattern he would follow for years to come.

"My man!" Malcolm would say when he'd meet a black inmate. "You ever heard about somebody named Mr. Elijah Muhammad?"

7

Out of the Darkness, Into the Light

ON AUGUST 7, 1952, Malcolm Little walked out of prison a free man, both mentally and physically. His conked hair had long since grown out and his head was covered with a tight cap of naturally coarse red curls. He'd developed eyestrain from endless hours of reading while in prison, and now had to wear eyeglasses. He looked like a different man from the one that had entered prison, and he was.

Malcolm spent his first night of freedom in Boston with Ella. She was glad to see him back out on the streets again, but his talk about Islam made her uncomfortable. Ella had no use for Islam.

The next morning, Malcolm traveled to Detroit where his brother Wilfred lived. Wilfred managed a furniture store in the black community of Inkster, Michigan, and he had convinced the owner to offer Malcolm a job once he was paroled. Wilfred had also invited Malcolm to live with him and his wife and children. Malcolm was grateful for both offers and humbly accepted them. He gave credit to Allah for these kindnesses.

Living in Wilfred's home gave Malcolm his first taste of daily Muslim living. All of the normal daily routines—rising, washing up, dressing, having breakfast, preparing for school or work—were carried out in a strict, orderly fashion that made each day get off to a smooth start.

As head of the family, Wilfred rose first, then his wife, and finally, the children. Wilfred was also the first to bathe and dress. The day itself was well ordered. Everything was scheduled around the five prayers Muslims make each day, facing their Holy City of Mecca.

Wilfred's children were very well disciplined, and both adults and children greeted one another in hushed tones at the new day's beginning. "As-Salaam-Alaikum" one would say, meaning "Peace be with you." And the other would reply, "Wa-Alaikum-Salaam," which meant "And to you be peace." After the harshness of prison life and the chaos of the hustling life, Malcolm appreciated the warm, loving, and stable atmosphere of Wilfred's home. It gave him a sense of wholeness and well-being. He felt ready to rejoin the world.

For Malcolm, that world now included Detroit's Nation of Islam Temple Number One. The Muslims met there on Wednesdays, Fridays, and Sundays. The women wore no makeup, Malcolm noticed. They wore modest ankle-length dresses, with matching scarves that covered their hair. The men wore neat but plain-colored suits and bow ties. The men and women treated one another with great respect, calling each other "Brother so-and-so" and "Sister so-and-so." Malcolm had never seen black men treat black women with honor before. He also noticed that the children at the temple were as well behaved as Wilfred's were at home.

On Malcolm's first visit to the temple, Minister Lemuel Hassan lectured for an hour on the teachings of Elijah Muhammad. Malcolm listened intently to the teachings that had changed his life. But he was disturbed by the fact that the temple, which was in a small storefront, still had empty seats. He complained about it to Wilfred, saying that Muslims should work hard to win new Muslim converts. However, Wilfred and the other members had more of an "Insha-Allah", or "As God wills," attitude about it, trusting Allah to bring in new members "in His own time."

On August 31, Malcolm joined other temple members on a trip to Chicago to hear the Honorable Elijah Muhammad speak at Chicago's Temple Number Two. At last, Malcolm would see with his own eyes the man he thought of as his saviour. It was a moment he had dreamed of for a long time. But never in all his dreams had he imagined that the man whose teachings were so powerful, and whose message was so mighty, would be as small and soft-spoken as Muhammad turned out to be. As Elijah walked toward centerstage surrounded by Muslim bodyguards, the Messenger was barely visible.

"I have not stopped one day for the past twenty-one years," began Elijah Muhammad. "I have been standing, preaching to you throughout those past twenty-one years . . . this word and revelation of God—which will give life to you, and put you on the same level with all other civilized and independent nations and peoples of this planet earth. . . ." Elijah went on to talk about the "blue-eyed devil white man" who had kidnapped Original Man from Africa, and had stripped him of his language, culture, and even his name. This white devil, said Elijah, had brainwashed the black man so that he no longer knew who he was, or where he'd come from.

At the end of the talk, Elijah mentioned Malcolm by name, calling him "the strong brother" who had written to him every day while he was in prison. Elijah praised Malcolm's faithfulness and challenged him to continue in his devotion to Allah. Malcolm thought he could not possibly be more thrilled, but the true highlight of the day came later. He and his whole family were invited to share a meal at the home of the Messenger himself!

During the meal, Malcolm kept thinking about the empty seats back at the Detroit Temple. He believed that Elijah held the key that could free the mind and spirit of the black man and thought that many more blacks should have the chance to hear Elijah's teaching. But how could they hear the message if they never came into the temple? Malcolm was determined to find a way to get them there.

Malcolm asked Elijah how many Muslims should attend Temple Number One, and Elijah said "thousands."

"Sir," asked Malcolm, "What is your opinion of the best way of getting thousands there?"

"Go after the young people," said Muhammad. Malcolm nodded, certain that the Messenger was right.

Back in Detroit Malcolm devoted every evening to going out in the black community and "fishing" for converts. He'd go into the bars and poolrooms and stand on street corners talking to people, one on one, using the street language he knew so well. He knew that people might listen to someone who spoke their own language, and some of them did. Still, only a handful seemed interested in "the true knowledge" or in Elijah Muhammad and the Nation of Islam. Malcolm had to beg those few to come to a temple meeting, and even after they'd heard a lecture, only one or two would actually apply for Nation of Islam membership. Malcolm found the process of making converts very frustrating, but he didn't give up.

It was during this time that Malcolm received a certificate from N.O.I. headquarters in Chicago, giving him his "X". The "X" represented the unknown name of his original African ancestor. It replaced his "slave" name, or last name, Little, which was the name given his forefathers by white slave holders. One day, Elijah taught, God himself would give each Muslim a Holy Name. Until then, each Muslim would keep his "X."

Malcolm X worked faithfully to win new members to the Nation and, in a few short months, the membership of Temple Number One tripled. Elijah praised Malcolm's efforts and even visited the Detroit Temple himself. Still, Malcolm thought the membership was growing much too slowly.

In January 1953, Malcolm gave up his job at the furniture store and looked for work elsewhere. Between January and June of that year, he worked at the Gar Wood Factory, a company that made garbage-truck bodies, and on the Ford Motor Company assembly line in Detroit. Both jobs paid more than the furniture store had. But Malcolm's daytime work was never as important to him as his work for Elijah Muhammad and the Nation.

Malcolm and the other members of the Detroit Temple made frequent trips to Chicago to hear "the Messenger of Allah" speak. After each meeting they were honored guests at Elijah's home.

On one such occasion, Elijah said he needed more young ministers in the N.O.I. who were prepared to be leaders, and who were devoted to spreading the teachings of Islam across the country. Malcolm was surprised to learn that he was one of the young ministers Elijah had in mind. Up to that time, the idea of becoming a minister had never occurred to him. With his criminal background, Malcolm certainly didn't see himself as any sort of religious leader.

Detroit Temple Minister Lemuel Hassan began to encourage Malcolm to speak at temple meetings. Malcolm thought it was a great honor to speak before a group of people as a representative of the Honorable Elijah Muhammad, and used the opportunity to tell his brothers and sisters how he had become a Muslim.

That talk went quite well, and weeks later, Hassan urged Malcolm to speak again. He told Malcolm to choose any topic he wished and encouraged Malcolm to improvise his speech. Malcolm remembered some of his prison debates and decided to speak on Christianity and slavery—two subjects he'd read about and debated at Norfolk Prison Colony and at Charlestown.

"My brothers and sisters," said Malcolm, ". . . this blue-eyed devil has *twisted* his Christianity to keep his *foot* on our backs . . . to keep our eyes fixed on the pie in the sky and heaven in the hereafter . . . while *he* enjoys his heaven right *here* . . . on *this* earth . . . in *this* life!"

Malcolm believed everything he said with his whole heart, and spoke so forcefully that his words struck each person like a bolt of electricity. And the longer Malcolm spoke, the more he knew that he'd found his purpose in life—to expose the white man for the devil he was, and to teach his people the truth about their African heritage.

In June 1953, Malcolm was named Assistant Minister of Detroit Temple Number One. He gave up his daytime work and devoted himself fully to the ministry of the Nation of Islam. From then on, the Nation took care of Malcolm's basic living expenses.

America was at war in Korea at the time, and FBI agents came to Malcolm asking him why he hadn't signed up for duty. Malcolm convinced them that he didn't know the army would accept men with prison records. The FBI warned him that unless he registered immediately, they would arrest him and send him to jail. Malcolm took no chances. He went to the draft board that same day and filled out a form as a "conscientious objector," stating that going to war was against his Muslim religion. Weeks later, he received a notice that he would not have to go into the army after all.

Malcolm poured himself into the work of the ministry, sometimes walking the streets late at night, pleading with the men and women he would meet— men and women lost in booze and drugs, hustling and self-hatred—to accept the true knowledge about their "beautiful African selves." Sometimes he would be amazed by his own emotion.

Malcolm visited the home of Elijah Muhammad and his wife, Clara, regularly. One thing that drew Malcolm and Elijah together was the fact that both men had spent time in prison. Elijah was arrested in 1942 for refusing to register for the draft, the very reason the FBI had come after Malcolm. Elijah was sentenced to five years in prison, but had been paroled after three and a half years.

Malcolm learned that Elijah was born Elijah Pool, son of a Baptist minister, and that Elijah was from Sandersville, Georgia—the same state as the Reverend Earl Little, Malcolm's father. Born into a family of thirteen children, Elijah had been forced to leave school after the fourth grade so that he could work full-time to help the family. An older sister taught him what she could in the evenings when he came in from work. Apart from that, Elijah learned everything he knew from his own reading—just like Malcolm.

Elijah had been race conscious from his earliest years in school. As he grew older and worked on the farms and in the sawmills of Sandersville, he noted with anger that the white bosses frequently cursed their black workers. He politely asked his employers to fire him if they didn't like his work, "but just don't curse me," he would say.

In 1923, after he was married with two children, Elijah's white employer degraded him before all the other workers. To avoid trouble for his family's sake, Elijah moved them to Detroit. There, in 1930, he met "Master" W. D. Fard, whom the N.O.I. followers called "The Prophet." Fard taught Elijah about Islam, the "true knowledge," and "Yacub's History," which Elijah then passed on to the "Lost Sheep of North America." Fard was their Savior, their Redeemer, their Messiah—their Mahdi. He had come to redeem the black man and return him to his "true religion."

W. D. Fard trained Muhammad as a minister, helped him set up a University of Islam in Detroit, then went with him to Chicago to establish Temple Number Two. In 1934, Fard disappeared without a trace.

Malcolm sat with Elijah for hours on end, listening to this soft-spoken man talk about the history of the Nation of Islam, about the divine mission that Fard had given him, and of the difficult but glorious work that lay ahead to resurrect the black man of North America. Malcolm looked up to Elijah as a teacher, and as a god. "I worshiped him," he wrote in his autobiography.

Detroit Temple Number Two continued to grow through Malcolm's efforts. In fact, Malcolm was so effective as a recruiter and teacher that, in the winter of 1953, Elijah began sending Malcolm on short trips to Boston on a regular basis, so that Malcolm could set up a temple there.

A Boston Muslim named Brother Lloyd X invited people to his home to hear Malcolm speak. Malcolm preached on the horrors of slavery and the evils of the white man. He stirred up the rightful anger of his listeners and persuaded them to leave their white God and embrace the black God of the Honorable Elijah Muhammad. At the end of each talk, Malcolm invited his listeners to join the N.O.I. After three months, enough had joined to start up a temple. Malcolm's half-sister Ella was among them. Boston Temple Number Eleven was born, and Malcolm was its first minister.

While Malcolm was in Boston, he looked up his old friend Shorty. Shorty had heard that Malcolm had "turned religious," and wasn't sure he wanted to see the man he knew as "Red." When the two men met, Malcolm talked to Shorty about Islam until Shorty made it clear that he wasn't interested. Malcolm let the subject drop, and spent the remainder of his visit with Shorty laughing about old times. Malcolm saw several other hustlers he'd known in Roxbury, but didn't bother to talk to them about Islam. He knew they were no more interested in Islam than he would have been when he was a hustler.

By March 1954, the Boston temple was well established. Malcolm left Minister Ulysses X in charge, and Elijah moved Malcolm on to Philadelphia. That spring, Philadelphia's Temple Number Twelve came into being. Their membership grew even faster than the temple in Boston.

Malcolm had done a splendid job for Elijah Muhammad and, in June 1954, he was rewarded. Elijah appointed him minister of New York City's Temple Number Seven. It was the most important temple because it was in the largest and best-known black community in America.

Malcolm arrived in Harlem anxious to look up old friends as he'd done in Boston. He was particularly interested in finding Sammy the Pimp, and in meeting with his old numbers runner and one-time enemy, West Indian Archie.

It wasn't long before Malcolm learned that Sammy was dead, killed by someone in the underworld. As for Archie, he had turned into a sick, weak old man, no longer able to frighten a fly. He lived in a small room in the Bronx. Malcolm went to see him.

Archie opened the door and squinted at Malcolm, not recognizing him at first. Nine years had passed since he'd last seen Malcolm, and the new Malcolm looked quite different from the old. The person Archie had known as Detroit Red had a flaming-red conk, wore expensive silk suits, and definitely did *not* wear eyeglasses. But the man before him, in a business suit and carrying a briefcase, did seem familiar.

"Red!" said Archie finally, "I'm so glad to see you!"

The two men discussed their old feud. Malcolm said he was sure he'd bet on that number Archie had paid him for, and Archie admitted that he might have written the wrong number down on Malcolm's betting slip. Both men decided it no longer mattered who was right.

Malcolm shared his new faith in Islam and the teachings of Elijah Muhammad with Archie, and Archie listened with interest. Both men knew, though, that Archie was close to death. There was little chance that he would change his life now.

Malcolm visited all of his old night spots, only to learn that many of the hustlers he'd known were dead, addicted to drugs or alcohol, were in prison, or had gone insane. As he often did now, Malcolm praised Allah for saving him and for sending him the words of the Messenger. Malcolm believed that, except for Islam, he would have ended up just as lost and broken as all the other hustlers.

Once Malcolm had toured his old hangouts, he began building up Harlem's Temple Number Seven.

Malcolm was a powerful speaker, but he found it difficult to win new converts to Islam in Harlem. He had to compete with dozens of other nationalist groups doing their own recruiting. Malcolm needed a new way to get the Muslim message out.

First he had leaflets printed to advertise the temple's meetings. Malcolm and other temple members handed them out on street corners all over Harlem.

Next they'd find a crowd gathered by another group, blend in with the people at the back and talk to them about the Honorable Elijah Muhammad. On Sundays, they would wait outside Christian churches and, when church let out, pull their Christian brothers aside and preach to them a new gospel about the wonderful teachings of the Messenger.

All of these efforts were successful to some degree, but many people hesitated to join the Nation even though they agreed with Muhammad's teachings. The Nation's strict code of conduct kept them away.

Muslims did not eat pork, smoke cigarettes, drink alcohol, or use drugs. They could not dance, date, gamble, attend movies, watch sporting events, or take long vacations. They could not lie, cheat, or disobey the law unless a policeman asked them to do something that was against their Muslim religion. There were even rules that controlled their home life. Men were not to quarrel with their wives or abuse them in any way. Finally, no Muslim could have sex outside marriage. These were the reasons why many in Harlem, and elsewhere, refused to join the Nation of Islam.

Still, Temple Seven's membership slowly grew.

Malcolm traveled on N.O.I. business at least three days a week. On Wednesdays, he went to Philadelphia to teach at Temple Number Twelve, then on to Springfield, Massachusetts, to set up a temple. On Thursdays, he traveled to Hartford, Connecticut, to preach his message to an apartment full of local maids, cooks, and chauffeurs. Eventually, these meetings led to the opening of Hartford Temple Number Thirteen. Later he helped to establish a temple in Atlanta, Georgia. Perhaps he wondered what his

Georgia-born father would have thought about that temple, and about his son.

The Nation continued to grow in numbers, and grew in its appeal to a wider range of the black population. The membership began to include intellectuals attracted by the keen mind of the Nation's best read and most articulate minister—a man who could quote Socrates and Shakespeare—Malcolm X. Among this new membership was sister Betty Sanders, a nursing student. She joined Temple Number Seven in 1956.

Betty Sanders, who became Betty X, was born in Detroit and had studied education at Tuskegee Institute in Alabama. When Malcolm met her she was studying nursing at a New York City hospital, and teaching classes in hygiene to the female members of Temple Seven.

Malcolm had always made it plain to all the Muslim sisters he met at the various temples where he lectured that he had no interest in marriage. He was devoted to his ministry and felt that he was too busy to make time for a wife and family. Besides, he'd never been involved with a woman he wanted to marry. But there was something special about Betty. Malcolm started to keep an eye on her.

By now, Malcolm's tireless work for the Nation, his exciting preaching style, and his special relationship with Elijah Muhammad made him a well-known figure within the Muslim community, and within the FBI. They had sent black agents into the various Muslim temples for the first time in 1953, and had been keeping a file on Malcolm ever since. One of the ways the FBI kept informed about the Nation was by reading *Muhammad Speaks*, the N.O.I. newspaper Malcolm started in 1957. The small newspaper, sold on ghetto street corners, informed its readers of news in the various temples around the country, and gave Malcolm another outlet for spreading the teaching of Elijah Muhammad. However, few people in the general population of Harlem, or America, had ever heard of *Muhammad Speaks*, or of Malcolm X and the Nation of Islam.

That changed on April 4, 1957, when Harlem Muslim Johnson Hinton was beaten and jailed by New York police. Malcolm led a group of Muslim brothers to the police station and demanded that Hinton be taken to a hospital. A mob gathered behind him as Malcolm and his followers took up a vigil outside the hospital until doctors informed him that Hinton was receiving the best of care.

The following day, the *Amsterdam News*, one of America's largest black-owned weeklies, carried the story on the cover. Within the following weeks and months, articles about Malcolm X and the Nation of Islam started appearing in newspapers across the country. On July 18, 1957, the *Los Angeles Herald Dispatch* ran a story with the title "Young Moslem Leader Explains The Doctrine of Muhammadanism" (This is what some people call Islam.). The article quoted Malcolm as saying, "Islam is a flaming fire sweeping across the entire Dark World today." It went on to say that "Mr. X discussed one of the most . . . controversial religions in Harlem . . ." On November 2, the *Pittsburgh Courier* printed an article titled "Detroit Moslems Continue Growth." "Messenger Elijah Muhammad," it said, "the spiritual leader of America's fastest-growing group of Moslem converts . . . sent his fiery New York minister, Malcolm X, to represent him in Detroit . . . One of Muhammad's most devoted followers, Malcolm X . . . devotes 24 hours daily to spreading Muhammad's message among the Negroes of America, and organizing his followers into well-disciplined, fearless warriors for Allah . . ." These articles, and others like them, got everyone in Harlem talking about "those Muslims" and about the man who called himself "Malcolm X."

Malcolm was glad to have the opportunity to spread the message of Elijah Muhammad through the press, but Sister Betty X began occupying his thoughts as much as Elijah.

In the year that Betty had been attending Harlem's Temple Number Seven, Malcolm had learned that she was intelligent, well educated, and deeply devoted to Islam. One of the sisters at the temple told Malcolm that Betty's foster parents had been giving her money for nursing school. However, they threatened to cut off her support unless she left the Nation. As much as she needed their financial assistance, Betty refused to turn away from Islam. When they stopped giving her money, she began taking babysitting jobs between classes to help pay her own way. Malcolm admired her devotion.

Malcolm dropped in on Betty's classes from time to time, as he did with all the other classes at Temple Seven. He started asking her out, always finding some official excuse. He'd take her to a museum, for instance, and say that he wanted to teach her something that she could pass on to the sisters she taught at the temple. But in his heart, Malcolm knew that he was starting to think about what it would be like to have Sister Betty X as his wife.

Malcolm told Elijah that he was thinking about getting married and Elijah asked to meet Betty.

It was natural for teachers from each of the temples to visit Chicago for special classes, and Malcolm arranged such a visit for Sister Betty. He knew that she would be invited to Muhammad's house along with all the other visiting teachers, and would have a chance to meet Elijah, who could then "look her over."

Elijah thought well of Sister Betty and told Malcolm so. Elijah's blessing was the only green light Malcolm needed.

A few weeks later, Malcolm drove to Detroit to tell his brother Wilfred about his plans to marry. Then, on impulse, he pulled into a gas station, found a public telephone, and called Betty back in New York. "Are you ready to make that move?" he asked. That was Malcolm's way of asking Betty to marry him. She screamed and dropped the telephone. When she picked up the phone again, she said yes.

The next day she met Malcolm in Detroit and introduced him to her family. The day after, the two drove to Lansing, and were married by a justice of the peace. On January 19, they returned to New York and moved into an apartment in a two-family house that belonged to the Nation of Islam. Later that year, in November, Betty gave birth to a girl who they named Attilah. After Attilah's birth, they moved to a larger, seven-room house in Queens, which was also owned by the Nation.

Malcolm's new wife and baby brought him a joy he'd never known, but having a family did nothing to slow him down. He continued to spend most of his time teaching, preaching, and traveling on behalf of Elijah Muhammad. He made his first trip to Africa as Elijah's representative just seven months after Attilah's birth. He regularly made time in his schedule to meet with newspaper reporters. And, now that he was married, his "free" time was spent on "dates" with Betty, taking her to the opera or the theater, or playing with Attilah. Yet Malcolm had more energy than ever, because the love of his family gave Malcolm new strength.

Malcolm would need that strength in the days that lay ahead.

*During most of Malcolm's ministry, he operated un-
der the shadow of Elijah Muhammad (pictured over
Malcolm's shoulder). Here, at a Harlem street rally
in 1963, Malcolm confers with fellow Muslim minister James Shabazz.*

PHOTO BY ROBERT L. HAGGINS

8

Bearing the Message, Meeting the Masses

ON JULY 13, 1959, the image of an angry black man flashed across the television screens of America. His piercing eyes took aim at the audience from behind thin eyeglass panes. His mouth opened round like the barrel of a gun, shooting out words that richocheted off the TV screen like bullets. What kind of things was he saying? "Every time you see a white man, think about the devil you're seeing . . . the black man needs *today* to . . . throw off the slavemaster white man . . . by any means necessary . . . Hear how the white man kidnapped and robbed and raped the black man . . . his evil and his greed cause him to be hated around the world . . ."

The man on the television screen was Malcolm X, and this was the image of Malcolm that American television gave to the world.

The program, hosted by Mike Wallace, was a five-part special on "News Beat" on Channel 13 in New York. It was a report on the Black Muslims titled "The Hate that Hate Produced," and its main message was that Elijah Muhammad and the Nation of Islam were teaching black people to hate whites.

But hate was not what Malcolm was teaching his children at home. While he spoke publicly about the evils of the white man, about racial superiority and the separation of the races, at home Malcolm taught his children that all men are created equal. He taught them that they had the potential to achieve whatever they wanted to in life, that beyond placing blame on "the enemy," they needed to take responsibility for shaping their own futures.

As soon as the initial shock of the Mike Wallace television program wore off, newspaper and magazine reporters were on the telephone to civil rights leaders around the country, asking for their reaction. Malcolm X and the Nation of Islam were hit with an avalanche of rejection. They were called reverse racists, Communists, hate messengers, and black segregationists. Malcolm was troubled that these attacks came from his own people, and he burned to respond to them. However, Elijah Muhammad forbid Malcolm to speak out against other black leaders. Blacks fought against each other entirely too much as it was, and Muhammad did not want to be guilty of doing the same. Malcolm was forced to swallow his anger for a while.

In the weeks that followed Malcolm stayed on the telephone, taking calls from the news media and making calls to Elijah in Chicago, seeking his advice and instruction on which interviews, television and radio shows to accept or turn down. Most of the calls came from American cities, but some reporters called from as far away as Paris, France, and Stockholm, Sweden. Whether at home with Betty and the baby, or in the Muslim-owned restaurant next to Temple Number Seven, after the Mike Wallace special was aired, whenever the telephone rang, it was generally for Malcolm.

Among the journalists that Malcolm met at this time was Alex Haley, the author of *Roots*. Black journalist Haley first interviewed Malcolm for an article in the *Reader's Digest*. Many meetings and interviews were to follow over the next years, most of them friendlier than the talks Malcolm had with white reporters.

The conversations between Malcolm and white reporters were always heated. *Do you really believe that the white man is the devil?* one would ask. *What about Abraham Lincoln? He freed the slaves, didn't he?* And Malcolm would reply, "Lincoln's concern wasn't freedom for the blacks but to save the Union." *Why are you anti-Christian, Mr. X?* another would want to know. "Christianity is the white man's religion," Malcolm would answer. But the question reporters asked most often was *Why do you teach hate, Mr. X?* And that was the question that always made Malcolm angry. "As soon as the white man hears a black man say he's through loving white people," Malcolm would shoot back, "then the white man accuses the black man of hating him. What I want to know is how the white man, with the blood of black people dripping off his fingers, can have the audacity to be asking black people do they hate him. That takes a lot of nerve."

In the end, it didn't matter how well thought out or well spoken Malcolm's responses to the press were. Newspapers rarely printed what he'd actually said. Instead, they'd print whatever they felt would sell the most newspapers.

The FBI, who'd been investigating the Nation for

years, began sending more black agents into the N.O.I. to report on the organization in general, and on Malcolm in particular. However, after learning about the teachings of Elijah Muhammad firsthand, many agents converted to Islam themselves. Some quit their jobs at the FBI altogether, while others remained on staff and worked as double agents, giving Malcolm inside information about the FBI's plans concerning the Nation.

Malcolm had been aware of the FBI presence since he first joined the Nation and knew that both the telephone in the temple's restaurant and his home phone were being tapped. Malcolm was very careful about what he said and whom he trusted. Whether on the telephone or before a television microphone, Malcolm knew that when he spoke, people listened.

Black community leaders continued to denounce Malcolm and the Nation of Islam for promoting racial separation as a solution to the race problem in America. Elijah Muhammad finally got tired of accepting these attacks in silence. He gave Malcolm the go-ahead to strike back and, when he did, Malcolm accused civil rights leaders like Martin Luther King, Jr., of being "Uncle Toms."

"This twentieth-century [Uncle] Tom . . . He doesn't want to be black, he wants to be white. And he'll get on his bended knees and beg for integration . . . despite the fact that the attitudes and actions of whites are sufficient proof that he is not wanted . . . This Negro is sick."

Civil rights leaders across the country were outraged. No one had ever attacked them so bluntly before, and they were quick to fight back. Soon there

was a war of words between the Nation and everyone who considered themselves part of the Civil Rights
Movement. The news media printed every angry
word.

C. Eric Lincoln's book titled *Black Muslims in
America* was published at about this time, and it
added to the media's frenzy. *Life*, *Look*, *Time*, *News-
week*—every magazine in the country was doing an
exposé on "the Black Muslims." Malcolm hated being
called a Black Muslim because the name separated the
Nation from all the other millions of Muslims around
the world, and he believed himself to be part of that
larger body of believers. But the Black Muslim title
stuck.

With Elijah's permission, Malcolm began accepting
invitations to sit on radio and television panels with
selected civil rights leaders to debate the problem of
racism in America.

Malcolm was always outnumbered on these panels.
He would be faced with several scholars and civil
rights leaders, all waiting for an opportunity to attack
the Nation of Islam's philosophy and to tear apart Malcolm's arguments on the Nation's behalf. But whether
the topic was racial separation and the need for a black
nation-state or the rights of blacks to arm themselves,
Malcolm always had the last word. He usually had the
first word, as well.

"Good evening, ladies and gentlemen," the show's
host would begin. "Tonight, we have with us—" That
was as far as the host got. Malcolm would interrupt
and finish the introduction himself.

"I represent the Honorable Elijah Muhammad, the
spiritual head of the fastest growing group of Muslims

in the Western Hemisphere. . . .'' From that moment until the end of the program, the show belonged to Malcolm.

One of the issues raised during these debates was self-defense. Malcolm frequently spoke of a black man's constitutional right to arm himself, and he personally saw to it that the paramilitary arm of the N.O.I., called the Fruit of Islam, learned forms of self-defense such as judo and karate. Malcolm also openly praised African and Third World revolutionaries for violently overthrowing their colonizers. For these reasons, Malcolm was accused of provoking blacks to violence.

Whenever the issue was raised in a panel discussion or in an interview, someone would mention Martin Luther King, Jr.—Malcolm's chief philosophical rival. Malcolm never hesitated to use these opportunities to criticize King and other civil rights leaders who encouraged nonviolent protest.

"You can't take a black man who is being bitten by dogs and accuse him of advocating violence because he tries to defend himself from the bite of the dog,'' Malcolm said in an interview. "Most of the Negroes you see . . . talking about . . . 'suffer peacefully,' they mean suffer peacefully at the hands of the white man . . . Any Negro who teaches other Negroes to turn the other cheek is disarming that Negro . . . And men like King—their job is to go among Negroes and teach Negroes 'Don't fight back' . . . King is the best weapon that the white man, who wants to brutalize Negroes, has ever gotten in this country.''

All of these panel discussions, interviews, and television exposés brought greater numbers of people into the N.O.I. temples. Between 1952 when Malcolm first joined and 1960, the membership had grown from four hundred to ten thousand.

In order to take advantage of the interest in the N.O.I. that the media coverage had stirred up, the Nation began holding mass meetings around the country in places such as the Uline Arena in Washington, D. C., the St. Nicholas Arena in New York City, and the Coliseum in Chicago.

Like everything else about the N.O.I. in the early 1960s, these mass rallies were major news events. They were the first black-run meetings that whites were not allowed to attend. However, after a few rallies, Elijah opened the meetings to the white press. Later he ordered his ministers to reserve a whites-only section for the general white public. This section was always filled.

Everyone who came to the meetings was searched by a Muslim man or women, to check for guns or anything else that could be used as a weapon against Elijah Muhammad. In addition, tobacco and alcohol had to be left at the door.

The crowds, numbering thousands, were controlled by members of the Fruit of Islam, who saw to it that everyone entering the arena was seated in an orderly fashion.

In the beginning, Elijah Muhammad was the key speaker, but other speakers would be scheduled as well. New ministers, like Malcolm's brothers Wilfred and Philbert, would be announced at the beginning of the program. Then one of the more respected young ministers, like Louis X of the Boston Temple, would speak. Minister Louis X was a special protégé of Malcolm's, who would follow in Malcolm's footsteps as the key spokesman for the Nation of Islam in the years to come. He would play another role in history as well: Like several other ministers in the Nation, Louis X would one day turn against Malcolm. The betrayal of this man hurt Malcolm deeply. Today, that man is known to the world as Minister Louis Farrakhan.

After Minister Louis or another young minister spoke, Malcolm would be introduced. He would talk briefly to prepare the audience for Elijah.

"My black brothers and sisters," Malcolm would say, "no one will know who we are . . . until we know who we are! We never will be able to go anywhere until we know where we are! The Honorable Elijah Muhammad is giving us a true identity and a true position—the first time they have ever been known to the American black man!

"My black brothers and sisters, you have come from your homes to hear . . . America's *boldest* . . . most *fearless* . . . most *powerful* black man!" Malcolm was talking about Elijah Muhammad, but he could have been describing himself.

These mass rallies were huge successes and, when donations were collected from the audience, there was plenty of money to pay for the cost of the arenas and to invest in the work of further spreading Elijah's teachings. The money also helped to pay for Elijah Muhammad's trips to Muslim nations in Africa and the Middle East. After one such journey in 1961, he renamed the Nation's temples "mosques" after the other religious meeting places in the Muslim world.

In the midst of all the rallies, panel discussions, and public debates, Malcolm and Betty's second daughter, Qubilah, was born. Ironically, she was born on Christmas Day, a day Muslims do not celebrate.

Malcolm's relationships with his wife and children were the calm and stabilizing forces in his life. He didn't spend much time at home, but he was careful to give Betty and the children all the attention he could so that his relationship with them could grow. He took Betty to Duke Ellington concerts and to the opera. When he went out of the country, he called home three times a week, sometimes twice in a day. He'd tell Betty to look in the dresser where she'd find money and a letter or a poem that Malcolm had written especially for her.

Malcolm let his children know that they were special, too. When he came home from one of his trips, he'd swing his daughters in the air until they giggled. Then he'd plant himself in a chair, set them on his knees, and talk and play with them and make them laugh in a way his own father never had. Malcolm wanted his wife and children to know that they were as important to him as his work for the N.O.I.

Malcolm was in high demand as a speaker now. Though intellectuals found such teaching as "Yacub's History" totally laughable, and believed that integration was the only workable solution to the race problem in America, a lot of what Malcolm said still made sense, and people wanted to hear it. There was something about the way he spoke that shook people to their very souls.

In March of 1961 Malcolm was asked to address the Harvard Law School Forum. As he stood before the audience of student scholars and professors, he marveled that, only a few years before, he'd been a hardened criminal and a house burglar, planning robberies nearby in a Harvard Square apartment. Now here he was, with an eighth-grade education, about to address a room full of white Ph. D.s who were anxious to hear what *he* had to tell them.

"The Christian world has failed to give the black man justice . . . we have been America's most faithful servants during peace time, and her bravest soldiers during war time. . . . Still, white Christians have been unable to accept us as fellow human beings. . . ." As Malcolm spoke, the nearly all white audience leaned closer.

"A cup of tea in a white restaurant is . . . token integration. Token integration will not solve our problem. . . . After four hundred years here among the Caucasians, we are . . . convinced we can never live together in peace . . . there will be no peace . . . as long as twenty million so-called Negroes are begging for [their] rights. . . .

"Do justice by your faithful ex-slaves. Give us some land of our own right here, some separate states so we can separate ourselves from you. Then everyone will be satisfied . . . otherwise . . . your entire race will be destroyed and removed from this earth by Almighty God, Allah."

The audience at Harvard was shocked, but they were fascinated with Malcolm and all he had to say, and he was invited back to speak on several occasions. He spoke at other universities as well, and the college community began to have great respect for his keen intelligence and skill as a public speaker.

The Nation of Islam was expanding in every way possible. Its membership continued to grow and new mosques were springing up everywhere. Its mass meetings had standing room only. The number of Muslim-owned businesses was increasing. The Islamic university was overflowing with students. A new twenty-million-dollar Islamic center was planned. All in all, the rapid growth was too much for one man to oversee.

Elijah Muhammad, who suffered from bronchial asthma, found it increasingly difficult to handle the constant travel and the speaking engagements at rallies and still have time to make all the business decisions that were necessary to keep the Nation running smoothly. He became weak, coughed constantly, and had trouble catching his breath. Malcolm and the other ministers worried about Elijah's health. Eventually, Elijah's doctor recommended that he move to Arizona where the climate would be better for him. Elijah followed his doctor's advice. The Nation bought him a house in Phoenix, and Malcolm was happy to learn that Elijah's health improved within weeks.

Elijah decided that the time had come to turn over more responsibility to Malcolm. He told Malcolm to start making more of his own decisions about which interview requests to accept, and to use his own wisdom in solving day-to-day organizational problems that might come up.

"Brother Malcolm," Elijah said to him one day, "I want you to become well known. Because if you are well known, it will make me better known. But . . . there is something you need to know. You will grow to be hated when you become well known . . . people get jealous of public figures."

Elijah Muhammad spoke the truth. What Malcolm couldn't have guessed is that, one day, Elijah himself would become the most jealous person of all.

In 1963 Malcolm walked through the streets of Harlem surrounded by Muslim ministers and members
of the N.O.I. Many of these ministers would later
betray Malcolm. They include Minister Louis Farrakhan, pictured here to the right and behind Malcolm,
looking up. The street, 115th and Lenox Avenue, was
renamed Malcolm X Boulevard.

PHOTO BY ROBERT L. HAGGINS

9

Trouble in the Temple

IN LATE 1961, the jealous rumors about Malcolm had begun. "Minister Malcolm is trying to take over the Nation," some people whispered. "He's taking credit for Mr. Muhammad's teaching," said others. Lesser known ministers accused Malcolm of building an empire for himself. "Minister Malcolm just loves playing coast-to-coast Mr. Big Shot," they complained. These things were all said behind Malcolm's back, but the gossip eventually got back to him.

The jealous whispers upset Malcolm because they were untrue. If anyone gave Elijah Muhammad credit for his teachings, it was Malcolm. In every speech or interview he gave, Malcolm began by saying, "The Honorable Elijah Muhammad teaches . . ." He said it so often, in fact, that reporters teased him about it. Malcolm even carried photographs of Muhammad in his briefcase and, at the end of an interview, would offer them to reporters, asking that the editor use Muhammad's photograph in the article rather than one of himself.

The truth is, Malcolm gave Muhammad entirely *too much* credit. On more than one occasion, Malcolm insisted that Elijah Muhammad had taught him everything he had learned beyond the eighth grade. Actually, Malcolm was largely self-taught. His endless hunger for knowledge and the long hours he spent reading to satisfy it were responsible for his homemade university-level education. Yet according to Malcolm, all praise was due to Elijah Muhammad.

But it was Malcolm X that the general public wanted to hear. Malcolm was particularly popular with college students. He spoke at Brown, Yale, Columbia, Rutgers, Clark, and Howard universities, among others. Elijah grew jealous of Malcolm because of Malcolm's ability to speak comfortably before such highly educated audiences.

By now Malcolm had grown tired of the way the press pitted him against civil rights leaders. He had criticized civil rights leaders in the past himself, of course. But now Malcolm realized that this was the wrong thing to do. Whether he agreed with men like James Farmer or Martin Luther King, Jr., or not, they were still his black brothers. And they were fighting for a better life for black people, just as he was.

Malcolm began to find ways to sidestep the press's efforts to goad him into saying something against King or other black leaders. Rather than focus on actions of specific civil rights leaders, Malcolm began to stress the crimes of the white man that led up to those actions. For example, when they asked him to comment on the Montgomery bus boycott let by King, Malcolm talked about how terrible the white man was for arresting a peace-loving, Christian black woman like Rosa Parks just because she refused to give up her seat in the front of a bus.

As Malcolm's fame grew outside of the Nation, forces

within the Nation itself tried to play it down. Malcolm's name appeared less and less in *Muhammad Speaks*, the Muslim newspaper that Malcolm had started. Eventually, on orders from Elijah's son Herbert, *Muhammad Speaks* stopped printing stories about Malcolm altogether.

Malcolm was hurt by this, but he accepted it because he knew that the orders came from the Nation's Chicago headquarters. Elijah Muhammad must have approved of the action, and Malcolm was not about to criticize the man to whom he felt he owed his life.

There were two bright spots in Malcolm's life that year. The first was the birth of his third daughter, Ilyasah. The second was meeting a young up-and-coming boxer named Cassius Clay.

Cassius Clay had read about Malcolm in newspapers and magazines, and had seen his picture often enough to recognize him. When Cassius and his brother Rudolph attended a Muslim rally at the Detroit mosque where Elijah Muhammad was speaking, Clay walked right up to Malcolm and introduced himself. He grabbed Malcolm's hand and shook it firmly. "I'm Cassius Clay," he told Malcolm. Malcolm was impressed by Clay's warmth and self-confidence. The two men liked each other immediately. After that first meeting, Clay made a point of going to hear Malcolm speak whenever his fights took him to a town where Malcolm's lectures were scheduled.

Malcolm enjoyed his new daughter and his new friend. Yet 1962 ended on a bad note. In December he began to hear a new kind of rumor. This new report was more shocking than the rumors about himself, and more disturbing. It was about Malcolm's idol, Elijah Muhammad. People were saying that Elijah, a sixty-seven-year-old married man, had gotten several of his former secretaries pregnant.

Malcolm could not treat this rumor as nonsense because several ministers from the Chicago Mosque had already left because of it. Moreover, the gossip began to spread among Muslims and non-Muslims alike. People would approach Malcolm when he was out teaching or speaking at rallies and ask him if he'd heard about "it," and if "it" were true. Malcolm pretended not to know what they were talking about, but he had nightmares about seeing the ugly rumor in the newspaper headlines.

Malcolm got the feeling that everyone knew more about what was going in the Nation than he did, and he hated it.

A call from Alex Haley took Malcolm's mind off the rumor for a while. The journalist told Malcolm that he wanted to write a book about Malcolm's life. Surprised, Malcolm first discussed the idea with Elijah. Elijah gave his permission, and work on the book, *The Autobiography of Malcolm X*, began. When Malcolm signed the book contract, he arranged for all of his profits to go to the Nation of Islam.

Malcolm's attention was soon drawn back to the rumors about Elijah, and Malcolm knew he could no longer ignore them. He decided to confront Muhammad. He called Chicago and told Elijah that he wanted to speak with him. Elijah seemed in no hurry to talk, though. He told Malcolm they could speak when they saw each other next. However, that meeting was several months away.

Meanwhile, Malcolm went to see Wallace Muhammad, Elijah's son, to discuss the matter with him. He and Wallace had always been especially close.

Malcolm wanted to discuss with Wallace ways that they could help his father, but Wallace said that Elijah wouldn't want any help. Malcolm thought that that was crazy and decided to take action on his own.

Malcolm located three of Elijah's former secretaries and interviewed them. They all confirmed that Elijah was the father of their children. They also let him know that Elijah had told them, and others in the Nation, that Malcolm was dangerous, and that Malcolm would turn against him one day.

The shock of learning about Elijah Muhammad's children born out-of-wedlock overwhelmed Malcolm. He decided to concentrate on Elijah's adultery and to try to forget everything else that he'd heard—at least for a while.

Malcolm knew that the news of Elijah's adultery would reach the press sooner or later and he feared that the scandal would destroy the Nation. He searched his mind for a way to explain Elijah's immoral conduct to his followers, a way to lessen the impact such a scandal could have.

An idea came to him. He could teach Muslims that a man's successes were more important than his personal failings. There were certainly enough examples of that belief in scripture. He and Wallace searched the Quran and the Bible for stories and parables that would support his idea. That way, Malcolm could say that Elijah's behavior was a fulfillment of prophecy.

Malcolm began teaching this philosophy in the New York mosques. Without mentioning adultery specifically, Malcolm stressed that a man's good deeds outshone his bad deeds.

Elijah Muhammad heard about these teachings, and finally sent for Malcolm in April.

Elijah and Malcolm hugged each other, like father and son. Malcolm talked frankly about the gossip, then talked about the plan he'd developed to explain Elijah's failing as the fulfillment of prophecy. He would compare the Messenger to King David, who was remembered for slaying Goliath, and not for committing adultery with Bethsheba. And he'd compare him to Noah, remembered for building the ark, not for getting drunk.

As Malcolm spoke, Elijah nodded. "Son, I'm not surprised," Elijah said finally. "You recognize that's what all of this is—prophecy. You have the kind of understanding that only an old man has. I'm David. When you read about how David took another man's wife, I'm that David. You read about Noah, who got drunk—that's me. . . . I have to fulfill all of those things."

For a moment, Muhammad talked as if the "fulfillment of prophecy" teaching was real. But Malcolm told himself he was imagining things, and put the thought out of his mind.

Back in New York, Malcolm gathered six trusted ministers from East Coast mosques and told them everything. A few had already heard the stories. Now Malcolm explained the fulfillment of prophecy teaching and instructed them to use it if—or when—the scandal reached the press. However, Malcolm's good intentions backfired. People at Chicago headquarters accused Malcolm of spreading the rumor unnecessarily, and of making matters worse in the process. It was a war Malcolm simply could not win.

Under a cloud of criticism from Chicago, Malcolm continued to represent Elijah Muhammad to the best of his ability. In May he was interviewed by Alex Haley for *Playboy* magazine, and appeared on television

Malcolm visits friend Cassius Clay (aka Muhammad Ali) at Clay's fight camp in Florida in 1964. From left to right, Malcolm's wife Betty Shabazz, daughters Attilah, Qubilah seated on Malcolm's lap, Ali, and Malcolm's third daughter, Ilyasah.

PHOTO BY ROBERT L. HAGGINS

in an interview by famous black novelist/essayist James Baldwin.

But the jealousy of other ministers, particularly those in Chicago, was so severe that Malcolm turned down other magazine and television interviews. He did maintain his speaking schedule, though.

At street rallies held in Harlem, seven to eight thousand people came out to hear Malcolm. These rallies should have been a great triumph for him, but their success brought him little pleasure since Chicago N.O.I officials treated the rallies as though they were unimportant.

On July 3rd, Malcolm's worst nightmare came true. The news of Elijah Muhammad's adultery made headlines across the country. Two of Elijah's former secretaries were taking him to court for child support, saying that he was the father of their children.

Once the terrible truth stood out clearly, Malcolm admitted to himself that he'd heard hints of Elijah's behavior as far back as 1955. But he was so devoted to this man that he'd refused to accept such an ugly truth about him. Any other Muslim would be thrown out of the Nation in disgrace. That's what had happened to his own brother, Reginald. And that was why Reginald had called Elijah a hypocrite. At last Malcolm understood.

Thanks to his old hustler's instincts, Malcolm also understood that it was time for him to beware of danger. He had always believed that he would die a violent death at an early age. And as his fame grew and his followers increased in number, Malcolm knew that his enemies were growing in number, too. He was not surprised that summer when he read reports from the Associated Press that the Louisiana Citizens Council, a chapter of the Ku Klux Klan, had offered ten thousand dollars for his death.

Shortly after he read these reports, Malcolm joined Elijah Muhammad at a rally in Philadelphia. There Elijah named Malcolm the N.O.I's first national minister. "This is my most faithful, hard-working minister," said Elijah. "He will follow me until he dies."

This was the last time Malcolm and Elijah were seen together publicly.

On August 28th, Malcolm attended the historic March on Washington, but only as an observer.

Originally the March was an unorganized uprising of angry black people, ready to travel to the capital to demand their civil rights. But according to Malcolm, once frightened government officials called in "recognized" civil rights leaders to organize the March, it was gradually transformed into a massive show of force that had no teeth. Though it had started off as an all-black movement, it ended up as a racially mixed parade which frightened no one—least of all the officials in Washington. To Malcolm's way of thinking, the March was a giant fizzle.

But fizzle or no, the March on Washington was big news. Three months later, though, there was more important news to report. On November 22, President John F. Kennedy was assassinated.

All of America went into shock. JFK was very much loved by Americans, both black and white. Understanding that, Elijah Muhammad sent word to all his ministers to refrain from making comments about the assassination, if asked by the press.

On December 1, Elijah was scheduled to speak at New York City's Manhattan Center. He was unable to attend and instructed Malcolm to take his place. Malcolm's speech was entitled "God's Judgment of White America." He'd written the speech one week before the assassination.

During the question-and-answer session after his talk, someone asked Malcolm what he thought of the assassination. Without thinking, Malcolm answered that the hatred of white Americans was so widespread that it had finally led them to kill their own president.

The next day, Malcolm's comments were in newspapers across the country.

On December 4th, Elijah Muhammad suspended Malcolm from the Nation for ninety days because of his remarks about JFK's assassination.

Malcolm was crushed by the news. For twelve years, the Nation had been his family. Most of his brothers and sisters by birth were part of that family. Now Malcolm was suddenly an outsider, with no family at all. He was forbidden to speak on Elijah's behalf, forbidden to teach at his own mosque in New York City, and was treated as an outcast by the people he had known as his friends and trusted colleagues.

Malcolm refused to criticize Elijah. He treated his suspension as simple discipline. It was difficult, though. Here he was, suspended for ninety days because of a few words, by a man who had committed adultery not once, but several times. Yet Malcolm took his punishment in silence, telling himself that no matter what Elijah had done, Elijah was still the man who had saved his life.

Malcolm was counting off the days until he could return to the Nation, until he began to hear people speaking of him as rebellious. N.O.I officials in Chicago were spreading the word that Malcolm had purposely gone against Elijah's orders not to comment on

JFK's death. Worse, Malcolm got word that a Mosque Seven official was telling Muslims under him, "If you knew what the Minister [Malcolm] did, you'd go out and kill him yourself."

This wasn't an official order for Malcolm's death, but Malcolm was sure Elijah Muhammad knew that Mosque Seven officials were planting the idea that Malcolm needed to be killed. The fact that such talk continued to go on without any criticism from Elijah meant that he approved of it.

Malcolm believed in truth more than anything. But this truth nearly destroyed him. He could no longer deny the fact that his dearest idol had become his greatest enemy.

Malcolm's wife Betty was worried about him, and so was his doctor. The doctor saw the tremendous strain Malcolm was under and strongly urged him to get some rest. Cassius Clay, Malcolm's friend, made that possible.

In January 1964, Clay invited Malcolm, Betty, and their three girls to be his guests for a week at his training camp in Miami, Florida. Clay was preparing for a major fight with heavyweight champion Sonny Liston. Malcolm accepted Clay's invitation gladly, grateful to get away from the telephones and the press. He needed time to think.

Malcolm walked around in a fog of emotional despair during that week in Miami. He went through the motions of polite conversation, but couldn't remember much of what he said. All he felt was pain and disappointment, and all he could think about was how completely Elijah Muhammad had betrayed him.

Malcolm was not chiefly concerned about the death threats. He had been prepared to die for Elijah Muhammad from the very beginning. But Elijah had destroyed Malcolm's faith in him. Elijah's immoral acts, the lies that he was telling about Malcolm behind Malcolm's back, Elijah's willingness to punish others for their failings while he covered up his own sins—these were the things that broke Malcolm's heart and killed his faith in Elijah.

Malcolm finally understood that Elijah Muhammad was not a god, and Malcolm was no longer willing to die for him.

Sportswriters visiting Cassius Clay's training camp asked Malcolm about his suspension from the Nation. Malcolm told them that the suspension would be lifted in ninety days, but he no longer believed it. Looking back over the last year—the whispers about his being "rebellious," rumors about him wanting to "take over" the Nation, reports of orders for his death from within the Nation itself—Malcolm knew that his suspension was permanent. Elijah wanted him out of the organization one way or another. Malcolm's JFK comment was just an excuse to get rid of him without making Elijah look bad in the public eye.

At the end of the week at Clay's camp, Malcolm took Betty and the girls back home to Queens, then rejoined Clay in Miami. On the night of the big fight at Miami's Convention Hall, Malcolm prayed with Clay in Clay's dressing room. Then Malcolm joined the crowd in the auditorium of eight thousand, sat in seat number seven—his lucky number—and watched his friend beat Sonny Liston for the heavyweight title of the world.

The next morning at a press conference, Malcolm stood beside Clay as Clay announced that he was a Muslim. Eventually, Clay would change his name and become known to the world as Muhammad Ali, the greatest boxer of all time.

Malcolm returned to New York to learn that his death had been ordered by a Nation official in his own Mosque Seven. This was the first official order for Malcolm's death. The man who put out the order was a former assistant, and another former assistant was asked to carry out the order. However, the second man knew of Malcolm's devotion to the Nation and could not kill him. Instead, he revealed the plot to Malcolm. Malcolm thanked the man for sparing his life, but knew that others in the Nation would kill him without a second thought. The time had come for him to separate from the Nation.

Malcolm had devoted more than a decade to serving black people as a teacher, helping to raise their level of awareness about their history, their potential, their human rights. He was a recognized leader, but his foundation was the Nation of Islam. If he left the Nation, what would he base his leadership, his teachings, on? Malcolm spent weeks trying to find an answer.

Malcolm still believed that Islam was the right religion to meet the spiritual needs of the black man. Yet if he were to build a new organization, he felt that it should reach out to black men of all faiths. And he knew that the black man needed an organization that would encourage economic independence and political unity within the race. Building such an organization was a big challenge, but once Malcolm determined what was needed, he was prepared to give it a try.

On March 8, 1964, Malcolm announced his split from Elijah Muhammad and the Nation of Islam. On

March 12, he announced the beginning of his own organization, called Muslim Mosque, Incorporated.

The Nation responded to the announced split in a move that was swift and cruel. They told Malcolm and his family to leave their Queens home immediately, as the building belonged to the Nation of Islam.

Malcolm was shocked. Betty was not. For years, she had begged Malcolm to set aside money for the family to secure their future, but Malcolm had not wanted to be accused of misusing N.O.I funds. He was certain, he had told her, that the Nation would provide for his family should they ever need anything. But he was wrong. Now, with very little savings, Malcolm was being pushed out of the only home he and his family had ever known, and he had nowhere to go. Malcolm called his lawyer. He was not going to move without a fight.

On March 26, Malcolm attended a press conference in Washington, D.C., held by his longtime rival, Martin Luther King, Jr. After the conference, the two met for the first and last time. Both men were cordial and posed together for photographers. By now, Malcolm's attitude toward King had softened. He had grown to respect the civil rights leader as a man of action, and King had learned to respect Malcolm's deep love for black people, as well.

The membership of Muslim Mosque, Inc. grew daily. Large numbers of militant Muslims from Mosque Seven made their own break with the Nation and joined Malcolm. Non-Muslim blacks, including members of the black bourgeoise, joined Malcolm's Muslim Mosque, Inc., too.

Malcolm received letters, telegrams, and telephone

calls of support from around the country. Contributions rolled in from a wide range of people, dozens of them white. Some of these whites wanted to know if they could join the organization. Amazed and gratified, Malcolm explained that they could not join since Muslim Mosque, Inc. was an all-black organization. But he did thankfully accept their financial support.

Requests for speaking engagements poured in—twenty-two in one day alone! According to a *New York Times* poll, Malcolm was the second most popular speaker in America. The first was presidential candidate Barry Goldwater.

In the midst of the excitement surrounding Muslim Mosque, Inc., Malcolm continued to look over his shoulder. He knew that there were still Muslims around who were convinced that killing him would be a holy act. In addition, since the N.O.I had filed official papers to throw him and his family out of their house, Malcolm's struggles with the N.O.I were far from over. Malcolm decided it was time to file some important papers of his own. He called Alex Haley, who was still working on Malcolm's life story, and asked him to make a change in his book contract. Instead of sending Malcolm's profits to the N.O.I, Malcolm wanted them sent to Muslim Mosque, Inc. or, if Malcolm died, the money should go to his wife and children. The contract change was made soon thereafter.

Malcolm sensed that his split with Muhammad was a new beginning as well as an end. He wanted to start over again. Forming Muslim Mosque, Inc. was part of his plan. But Malcolm also felt the need for spiritual renewal. He decided it was time for him to make the pilgrimage to Mecca, the Muslim Holy Land. The only problem was that he didn't have the money for the journey.

Malcolm's half sister Ella had come to his aid so many times in the past. Malcolm wondered, could Ella help him now?

Malcolm boarded a plane for Boston to find out.

10

Hajj: A Letter from Mecca

AS ALWAYS, ELLA was glad to see Malcolm. She knew about his split from the Nation, of course. She'd long since left the Nation herself, and now studied under a group of Orthodox Muslims who lived in Boston. Ella had even started an Arabic-language school. She didn't know any Arabic, but she'd hired teachers who did. Ella felt it was important for true Muslims to understand the language in which the Muslim holy book, the Quran, was originally written. Like most American Muslims, Ella had to rely on English translations. At the very least, she wanted to learn enough Arabic to prepare for Hajj, a journey to the Muslim Holy City of Mecca, the place where the religion of Islam was born. According to the Quran, it was every Muslim's duty to make the pilgrimage once in his or her life, if at all possible.

Ella decided that her pilgrimage would have to wait. She believed it was more important for Malcolm to go. She gave him the money he needed and, as always, wished him the best. The next day, Malcolm returned to New York to prepare for the journey.

Malcolm went to the Saudi Arabian consulate to apply for a visa and learned that Muslims converted in America needed a letter of approval to get into Mecca. The man who had to write that letter was a United Nations advisor and a leading scholar on Islam named Dr. Mahmoud Youssef Shawarbi. Shawarbi, who had met Malcolm earlier, was glad to give Malcolm the letter he needed.

Shawarbi had something else for Malcolm as well. A man named Abd ar-Rahman Azzam had sent a copy of his book, *The Eternal Message of Muhammad*, to Shawarbi to pass on to Malcolm as a gift. Azzam had been following Malcolm's career in the press, Shawarbi explained. Azzam knew that Malcolm and Shawarbi had met, and that Shawarbi would know how to contact Malcolm. Malcolm was quite surprised, especially when he learned that Azzam was a close advisor to Prince Faisal, ruler of Saudi Arabia.

Malcolm accepted the book and thanked Shawarbi for the letter of approval. Shawarbi also gave him a letter of introduction and the phone number of his son Muhammad, who lived in Cairo, Egypt—Malcolm's first stop—and the number of Omar Azzam, the son of the author of *The Eternal Message of Muhammad*. Omar lived in Jedda, the last stop before Mecca. Shawarbi urged Malcolm to call on both men.

A few days later Malcolm slipped out of the country quietly, not wanting to draw attention to himself. Only Betty, the children, and a few of Malcolm's close associates saw him off at Kennedy International Airport.

On the plane, Malcolm sat next to two other Muslims, one who was on his way to Jedda, and the other who, like Malcolm, was headed for Cairo. The plane stopped in Frankfurt, Germany, where the man headed for Jedda said good-bye to Malcolm and caught another flight. Malcolm and the other gentleman went sightseeing in Frankfurt until it was time for their flight to Egypt.

Malcolm was very surprised to find that the people in Frankfurt, most of them white, were genuinely friendly toward him. He wasn't used to being treated kindly by white shopkeepers and salesmen, and he enjoyed the experience.

Malcolm and his new friend returned to the airport and got on a United Arab Airlines plane to Cairo. The flight was filled with Muslims from around the world, all on their way to the Muslim Holy Land. Malcolm saw people of every skin color imaginable, and was amazed at how well they all got along. Among this group of Muslims, Malcolm realized, there were no color problems.

In Cairo, Malcolm said good-bye to his seatmate. Malcolm wanted to do some sightseeing in Egypt before continuing to Saudi Arabia. The gentleman gave Malcolm his telephone number and told Malcolm to call before leaving Cairo. He wanted to put Malcolm in touch with a group of friends who were also on their way to make Hajj. Since Malcolm was traveling in the Arab world but didn't speak any Arabic, he needed someone to look out for him.

For two days, Malcolm toured Cairo, visiting the great pyramids and other historical sites. Finally he contacted Dr. Shawarbi's son, and the two met for lunch. Then, when Malcolm was ready to continue his journey, he called the gentleman with whom he'd flown to Cairo. The man introduced Malcolm to his friends, and Malcolm joined their party. They were excited to be making Hajj with an American Muslim, and they treated Malcolm like a brother from the start.

Unfortunately, they were not able to make the pilgrimage with Malcolm after all. When the group reached Jedda, Hajj officials at the airport pulled Malcolm aside. Since he was American, and there were relatively few Muslims in America, Hajj officials wanted to make sure he was a true believer in Islam. Only true Muslims were allowed into the Holy City of Mecca. Malcolm would have to go before the Muslim High Court for questioning. They would decide whether he was a true Muslim or not.

One official took Malcolm's letter of approval and his passport. Another official, a Hajj guide, took Malcolm to a dormitory beyond the airport to wait for his turn to go before the High Court. At the dorm, Malcolm met other non-Arab Muslim converts who were waiting for approval to enter Mecca. There were people from such places as Indonesia, Japan, Russia, China, and Afghanistan. Malcolm, somewhat in a daze, was taken to a compartment with fifteen other people. He didn't speak their languages, and they didn't speak his. He felt confused and foolish, and nervously wondered if he would get to make the pilgrimage after all.

Malcolm decided to try to communicate with his roommates. A man from Egypt seemed particularly friendly. He came over to Malcolm and said "hello." Malcolm was thrilled to hear a word of English. He asked the man his name, but soon realized that the man did not understand him. The man's English was limited to ten or twenty words. Still, Malcolm was not discouraged. If nothing else, Malcolm knew he was a good teacher.

Malcolm pointed to various things around the room, telling the Egyptian what they were in English, and urging the man to repeat the words after him. "Rug

. . . sandal . . . foot . . . eyes . . ." and so on. Finally, Malcolm mentioned the name of someone the Egyptian might have heard of. "Muhammad Ali Clay," said Malcolm. "He's my friend." The Egyptian's eyes lit up. Like most people, he had heard of the new heavyweight champion of the world. The man became very excited. He thought Malcolm was Muhammad Ali. Malcolm tried to explain that he was Muhammad's *friend*, but he couldn't tell if the man understood.

Word quickly spread that Malcolm was a Muslim from America. People were especially kind to him after that. Everyone wanted to protect him. Malcolm felt like an honored visitor from Mars.

Malcolm's Hajj guide came every few hours to take Malcolm to the local mosque for prayers. He showed Malcolm the proper way to do the ritual washing before prayers, to kneel, and to sit on the prayer rug. He also led Malcolm in prayer in the Arabic language. Malcolm was embarrassed to be a minister of Islam in his country, and to not know these things. He made up his mind to correct his weaknesses.

After the evening prayer, Malcolm remembered that Abd ar-Rahman Azzam, the author of *The Eternal Message*, had a son living in Jedda. Perhaps the younger Azzam could help Malcolm get approval to enter Mecca. Malcolm ran to Hajj officials and asked them to call Azzam for him.

Within the hour, Omar Azzam arranged for Malcolm's release, got his suitcase and passport, and picked him up. Omar scolded Malcolm for not calling sooner. He was upset that this man, whom his father highly respected, should have spent the night sleeping on the floor in a dreary room crowded with fifteen other people.

Malcolm was relieved to have someone to talk to in English. He felt less alone now, and he could not get over the fact that this man with white skin, who was a total stranger to him, treated him like a long-lost brother.

Omar Azzam took Malcolm to his home. During the ride, Malcolm learned that Omar was the brother-in-law of Prince Faisal's son. Malcolm could hardly believe that he was sitting next to a relative of the ruler of Saudi Arabia. Omar also informed Malcolm that his father, Abd ar-Rahman, was in town and was anxious to meet Malcolm. The elder Azzam would be staying with his son so that he could loan his suite at the Jedda Palace Hotel to Malcolm while he was in town. Malcolm was overwhelmed.

At Omar's home, Malcolm met Abd ar-Rahman, as well as Omar's uncle and a close friend. Each man hugged Malcolm warmly, fussing over him to make sure he was comfortable. Later, Malcolm was taken to the Jedda Palace Hotel to rest.

One of the first things Malcolm did when he got to the hotel suite was fall on his face and pray. He had much to be thankful for. The letter and telephone numbers from Shawarbi, the assistance of Omar Azzam, the generosity of Omar's father, the luxurious hotel suite—all the result of kind, *white* strangers.

Later that evening Malcolm had dinner with Dr. Azzam and his son. They informed Malcolm that he was to go before the Hajj Committee Court the following morning.

The Hajj judge asked Malcolm a series of questions about his faith and determined that Malcolm was a true believer. The judge then gave him two books on Islam, and entered Malcolm's name in the Holy Register of true Muslims. At last he was free to make the pilgrimage as planned.

Malcolm returned to the hotel for lunch, then slept for a few hours. He woke up when the telephone rang. The call was from the Deputy Minister of Protocol for Prince Faisal. Prince Faisal, supreme ruler of Saudi Arabia, was sending a car for Malcolm after dinner. The chauffeur and another man would escort Malcolm to Mecca and return him to Jedda once his Hajj was complete.

Malcolm was speechless.

Early that evening, after a short drive on the turnpike, Malcolm entered the ancient city of Mecca. A Hajj guide waved the car over and motioned the driver to park near the Great Mosque. There, Malcolm washed according to ritual. He removed his sandals and followed the guide to the center of the Mosque where a giant black stone house, called the Ka'ba, sat. "God is great!" Malcolm cried out when he saw the Ka'ba. Then he joined the thousands of pilgrims who circled the Ka'ba seven times. He prayed, then went to the well called Zem Zem and took a drink. After drinking from the well, Malcolm joined other pilgrims as they ran between the hills of Safa and Marwa.

Malcolm returned to the Great Mosque twice more before the night was over, circling the Ka'ba seven times during each visit. The following day, he went to Mount Arafat, where he stood with thousands of Muslim brothers and sisters shouting praises to their God.

Finally Malcolm joined the crowd as each one threw seven stones at the devil, a ritual marking the end of Hajj. He joined twenty other Muslims who had just completed Hajj in a tent that had been set up on Mount Arafat. Since he was the only American present, everyone was curious to know what had impressed him most about Hajj. Someone who spoke English asked him. "The *brotherhood!*" said Malcolm without hesitation. "The people of all races, colors, from all over the world coming together as *one!*" This deep brotherly love and oneness was not only experienced by Muslims in Mecca. It existed at the heart of the Christian Church, too, but Malcolm had never personally experienced it in America. Now that he had seen with his own eyes that true faith could make even white-skinned people color-blind, he began to rethink his ideas about the white race.

Malcolm wrote several letters about his experience in Mecca to close friends and associates. He sent one to his Muslim Mosque, Inc. assistants, asking that they copy the letter and send it to the press. The first person he wrote to, though, was his wife Betty. "Never have I witnessed such sincere hospitality and the overwhelming spirit of true brotherhood, practiced by people of all colors and races here. . . . If white Americans could accept *in reality* the Oneness of God . . . perhaps . . . they could accept *in reality* the Oneness of Man . . ."

Malcolm signed the letter "El-Hajj Malik El-Shabazz." He'd used the name Malik on earlier trips to the Muslim world. Now he could add to that name the title of Hajj, for his pilgrimage was complete.

Malcolm caused excitement everywhere he went. He was the famous Muslim from America. But many of the people Malcolm was to meet during this trip were far more famous and powerful than he.

While still in Mecca, Malcolm met the Muslim religion's highest official in Jerusalem, the Grand Mufti.

He also met members of the Turkish parliament, and the mayor of Mecca.

Back in Jedda, Malcolm met a variety of African officials in the lobby of the hotel. Numbers of them, he discovered, had followed his career in the international press. He held several informal talks in that lobby, preaching about the evils of American racism and the need for newly independent African nations to support their struggling African brothers in America. And, as government officials from Sudan and India hugged him and called him brother, Malcolm realized that American blacks should no longer think of themselves as a minority, but should understand that, as part of the nonwhite population of the world, African-Americans are part of the *majority*.

Malcolm's time in Jedda was almost up. Before he left, he was invited to meet Prince Faisal himself.

The prince stood up to greet Malcolm when he entered Faisal's office. The two shook hands warmly, and Faisal offered Malcolm a seat. An interpreter translated their conversation.

Prince Faisal asked several questions about the Black Muslims. He'd read articles about them and said that the version of Islam the Black Muslims were teaching was all wrong. Malcolm explained his past relationship with the Nation, and that he had recently split from them. He had made Hajj, Malcolm told the prince, so that he could learn more about the true religion. As the visit ended, Faisal mentioned that there were dozens of fine books on Islam written in English for any student of Islam who was sincere, as he believed Malcolm was. With that, the meeting was over.

At the end of April, Malcolm left for Beirut, Lebanon, and spoke at the American University. Next he flew to Nigeria, where he was guest speaker at Ibadan University. He told his audience that blacks in America were fighting for civil rights, but that they weren't receiving even their human rights. Free African nations such as Nigeria, Malcolm told them, should help their American brothers bring the issue of black American human rights before the United Nations for discussion.

Malcolm appeared on Nigerian radio and television while he was there, and was treated with a dinner given in his honor. He never felt more like a prince. But it was in Ghana, Malcolm's next stop, that he was truly given the royal treatment.

When Malcolm arrived in Accra, Ghana, he found a committee of black Americans waiting for him. They were a group of forty blacks who were living in Ghana at the time, and included authors Julian Mayfield and Maya Angelou. Malcolm was impressed at the size of this "Malcolm X Committee." Yet there were greater surprises in store for him.

Newspapers in Ghana had been covering Malcolm X and the Nation of Islam for years. Press officials were thrilled about Malcolm's visit and had arranged to pay for his hotel. He was asked to speak at a Ghanaian press conference where he told listeners that the destinies of Africans and African-Americans were tied together.

Aside from the press conference, a variety of lunches, dinners, and parties were given as a tribute to Malcolm by ambassadors from Nigeria, Algeria, Mali, and China. Malcolm met and spoke with government officials from around the world at these events, including Ghana's minister of defense, and the ambassador of Cuba.

American officials were horrified to see how much high regard world leaders had for Malcolm. The American ambassador to Ghana was careful to be particularly friendly to Malcolm during his stay, but Malcolm—and the Ghanaians'—knew that the man was only putting on a show.

Malcolm learned that Muhammad Ali was due to arrive in Ghana. Malcolm hadn't been in contact with his old friend since Malcolm split from the Nation of Islam. As Ali was still a follower of Elijah Muhammad, Malcolm felt that a meeting with Ali might be awkward for them both. He decided to avoid running into Ali, if at all possible.

Between the press conferences and official banquets, Malcolm met Ghana's president, Kwame Nkrumah. Of all Africa's leaders, it was Kwame Nkrumah who most believed in Pan-Africanism—the idea that all people of African descent are culturally and politically linked. For this reason, meeting Nkrumah was a high point of Malcolm's visit to Ghana.

On the day that Malcolm left Ghana, five of the ambassadors he'd met drove to the airport to see him off. It was quite an honor.

From Accra, Malcolm flew to Liberia, then to Senegal. In Dakar, Senegal, people lined up at the airport to shake Malcolm's hand and to get his autograph.

On May 19, his birthday, he flew to Algiers. He was thirty-nine years old.

Two days later Malcolm arrived back in New York and faced a crowd of reporters and photographers.

While Malcolm was on Hajj, several young blacks

had been accused of killing a white storeowner in Harlem. Unproven reports said that these youths were Black Muslims who had left the N.O.I to join Malcolm's organization. Was it true? reporters asked. Why had he once commented that blacks should form rifle clubs? They hinted that such comments were to blame for black violence against whites. The issue of blacks being armed was in the newspapers regularly, because the ghetto riots of the long, hot summer of 1964 had already begun to break out across the country. Malcolm had predicted such an explosion of violence. Now white Americans wanted to blame him for inciting that violence.

Malcolm sighed, thinking about how familiar the reporters' questions and accusations were. He had come back to America a new man. But America, Malcolm was quickly reminded, was the same hate-filled country it had been when he left.

Malcolm answered the reporters' questions, assuring them that he knew nothing about the men accused of killing the white storeowner, and reminding them that blacks had the constitutional right to bear arms to defend themselves.

Reporters also asked Malcolm about his "Letter from Mecca." Did the letter mean that he no longer hated whites? Malcolm answered that, after his experience in Mecca, he could no longer judge all white people as being the same. In the future, he would judge individual whites based on how that individual treated his black brothers. Malcolm was convinced that some American whites did want to rid the country of racism—but they were not in the majority.

Malcolm made a few more statements to the press,

then went home to his wife and children. He needed a good night's sleep. There was work to do.

Malcolm had a new vision for Black America, a new plan of action to help his people win their rights. He knew it would take every ounce of his strength to bring that vision to life.

11

O.A.A.U.: A Fragile Beginning

MALCOLM HAD CHANGED and he wanted everyone to know it. After his return from Hajj, he held meetings at Harlem's Audubon Ballroom each Sunday, where he spoke to non-Muslim black audiences. He told them that they were all black people with a common experience, a common cause. It didn't matter if they were Muslim or Christian, Democrat or Republican. "True Islam taught me that it takes all of the religious, political, economic, psychological, and racial ingredients, or characteristics, to make the Human Family and the Human Society."

Malcolm addressed white audiences differently now, too. "I don't speak against the sincere, well-meaning, good white people," he said. "I have learned that there *are* some. I am speaking against . . . the white *racists*."

The most important change for Malcolm, personally, was that he rejected the religious teachings of Elijah Muhammad. Now Malcolm believed that there was no God but Allah, and that an Arab prophet named Muhammad ibn Abdullah, who lived fourteen

158

hundred years ago in the city of Mecca, was the true last Messenger of Allah—not Elijah.

Yet even if he talked about the importance of black unity, or his new ideas concerning white people, or his new religious beliefs, the media still continued to picture Malcolm as the "angriest man in America."

Malcolm found it almost impossible to change his public image. With black ghetto riots breaking out all over the country, newspapers repeatedly accused Malcolm of teaching violence and stirring up black hatred of whites. After all, they reminded the world, Malcolm had been the one to suggest that blacks arm themselves, that they learn self-defense, that they fight for their rights "by any means necessary." If it weren't for such "Black Muslim teaching," reporters insisted, there might not be any riots in the streets. Malcolm still believed in active self-defense, but he wasn't telling anyone to riot. The fact that white racists chose to blame him for the riots rather than admit—even to each other—that they had caused the trouble themselves made Malcolm angry.

He didn't give up trying to change his public image, though. Malcolm knew he had to convince people that he was sincere, that he had truly changed direction. He was determined to build a new organization uniting all blacks to help create a society of true brotherhood between blacks and whites—the same goal Martin Luther King, Jr., had spoken of in his famous "I Have a Dream" speech.

Malcolm and King had grown closer in their ideology than anyone would have dared to imagine.

A handful of black people were prepared to accept the new Malcolm, and they formed the core of his new group, the Organization of African-American Unity. Apparently, this organization replaced Muslim Mosque, Inc.

The O.A.A.U., as it was called, was formed in the living room of black historian John Henrik Clark. Malcolm, Clark, and the others at the meeting agreed that the organization should help the black community work toward economic self-reliance and self-defense, that it should encourage high moral standards of living within the black community, and that it should provide strong spiritual direction.

Malcolm officially announced the formation of his O.A.A.U. on June 28, 1964. The purpose of the group, he told the press, was to unite all African-Americans to fight for their human rights. Malcolm admitted that every black organization—including the N.A.A.C.P.—had something to contribute to the black struggle. Malcolm and his O.A.A.U. were prepared to join forces with selected black leaders.

The main focus of the O.A.A.U. was to get blacks to view the problem of racial discrimination as an issue of universal human rights, and not just as a North American civil rights problem.

On July 9, eleven days after setting up the new organization, Malcolm returned to Africa. While he was there, he attended the African Summit Conference as a representative of the O.A.A.U., asking officials from thirty-four African nations to discuss the cause of black Americans at the United Nations. Malcolm also met with the presidents of Egypt, Nigeria, Tanzania, Kenya, Uganda, and Guinea. He met with a number of religious leaders as well, traveling from country to country, building bridges between African-Americans,

Africans, and the nonwhite peoples of the Middle East and Asia.

Malcolm was in Africa eighteen weeks all together—much too long as far as members of his new organization were concerned. While Malcolm had been busy developing international links, the O.A.A.U. was left without a leader. Key members were becoming disillusioned, wondering if Malcolm was interested enough in the organization to make it work, while other people in Harlem complained that all Malcolm ever did was talk. When was the O.A.A.U. going to *do* something? they wanted to know.

Malcolm knew a lot was expected of him by black people in general, and O.A.A.U. members in particular. But he owed something to his wife and family, too. This latest separation had been particularly hard on Betty. Lawyers for Malcolm and the Nation of Islam were still battling to decide whether Malcolm had a right to continue living in a house owned by the N.O.I. On September 1, while Malcolm was in Africa, the legal battle was settled. The court ordered Malcolm and his family to move out by the following January. Malcolm regretted not being home with Betty when the terrible news arrived.

Malcolm returned to New York on November 24, knowing that he needed to raise a lot of money in a short amount of time. He needed cash for personal expenses, to hire a full-time O.A.A.U. official, and to cover the rent on the O.A.A.U. office at Harlem's Hotel Theresa. To meet these needs, he began a hectic schedule of speaking engagements that kept him busier than ever before. He was on the go an average of eighteen hours a day.

The first speaking date he accepted after his return from Africa took him to London, England, to participate in a debate at Oxford University. It was scheduled six days after he'd stepped off the plane from Algiers. This time, though, Malcolm was gone for only a few days.

In December, in the midst of a whirlwind of travel and speechmaking, Malcolm happily welcomed his fourth daughter, Gamilah, into the world.

The world that Gamilah came into was growing more violent every day, and that violence touched her family directly. By the end of 1964, Malcolm was using every opportunity to publicly expose Elijah Muhammad and the N.O.I as religious fakes. As he did so, death threats against him multiplied. Threats were called in to police stations, newspapers, the O.A.A.U. office and Malcolm's home. Betty had the home phone disconnected so that the family could get a rest from the hate-filled calls.

During the same period, Malcolm was scheduled to speak in Boston, but was unable to go. Rather than cancel, he sent an O.A.A.U. assistant to speak in his place. After the lecture, the assistant headed for the Boston airport to return to New York. The car he was in was blocked by a second car. According to reports, several men wielding knives stormed the car, thinking that Malcolm was inside. When an O.A.A.U. member in the first car showed his shotgun, the attackers ran away.

Malcolm stepped up his security after that incident, making certain that Betty knew how to use the rifle that Malcolm kept in the house. In addition, he called Alex Haley and suggested that he and Haley rush to finish the book on Malcolm's life that they were working on together. "I'm a marked man," Malcolm told Haley. "If I'm alive when this book comes out, it will be a miracle."

The fact that Malcolm had survived the torching of his childhood home, hunger during the Great Depression, foster homes, detention homes, street hustling, and prison was a miracle in itself. How many miracles did Malcolm have left? Nobody knew for certain.

On December 13, 1964, on the stage of the Audubon Ballroom, Malcolm shares a laugh with Abdul Mohammad Babu, leader of the 1964 revolution in Zanzibar, East Africa.

PHOTO BY ROBERT L. HAGGINS

12

Fallen Star

TIME WAS PRECIOUS to Malcolm and he rarely wasted it. One day early in January 1965 Alex Haley called Malcolm from New York's Kennedy Airport. Haley had just flown in from Kansas, on his way to upstate New York, and told Malcolm that he had some time between flights. Malcolm immediately decided to take advantage of it. He drove to Kennedy and met Haley to discuss details Malcolm wanted to add to his autobiography.

Malcolm talked about the frustration of trying to change his image. "They won't let me turn the corner!" he said. "I'm caught in a trap." The men discussed politics for a while, then turned to the subject of Malcolm's family. Betty was pregnant again and Malcolm laughed about having had four daughters in a row. He was sure, he said, that the next child would be a boy. "If not," said Malcolm, "the *next* one!" Haley smiled at his friend, then checked the time. His plane was leaving soon. He stood up to leave.

The two men shook hands warmly and said goodbye. It was the last time Alex Haley saw Malcolm alive.

Malcolm continued to be seen by a lot of other people, though. On January 19, Malcolm was a guest on a television show in Canada. Someone on the program asked Malcolm his opinion of marriage between people of different races. Malcolm said that people of all races are human beings, and that human beings have a right to decide who they wish to marry. The television audience was amazed. Anyone who had followed Malcolm's career knew that he had come a long way from his early teaching of racial separation during his years with Elijah Muhammad. Malcolm's thinking had changed so radically since his N.O.I. days that, to him, those days seemed like another lifetime.

Malcolm couldn't get too far away from his past, though. The Nation wouldn't let him. Whenever he was in America during the latter months of 1964 and early 1965, members of the N.O.I. turned up at the hotel where he was staying or the television or radio studio where he was taping a show. They seemed to know his schedule better than he did.

On January 28, Malcolm flew to Los Angeles to meet with two of Elijah Muhammad's former secretaries and their lawyer. These were the two secretaries who had filed suit against Muhammad for child support in July 1963. Their cases were still being tried in court, and Malcolm agreed to meet with their lawyer. Malcolm offered her information about Muhammad's conduct with other former secretaries.

Members of the Nation of Islam, angry about this meeting, surrounded Malcolm's hotel. When Malcolm left the hotel for the meeting, he bumped into six Black Muslims in the lobby. Malcolm tensed, sensing trouble, but kept walking. A special police intelligence squad assigned to Malcolm watched the scene. Nothing happened.

166

That evening, Malcolm met two friends for dinner. When they drove back to his hotel, they saw Black Muslims everywhere, in cars and on foot. Malcolm jumped out of the car and raced into the hotel lobby. He went directly to his room and stayed there until it was time to go to the airport.

The drive to the airport was tense. Two carloads of Muslims followed Malcolm. The cars sped up, coming closer to Malcolm's car. Malcolm was sure the men had weapons. He grabbed his friend's cane and stuck it out a rear window, holding it like a rifle. The two cars fell behind instantly, and Malcolm reached the airport without incident. Police met Malcolm and escorted him to the plane. Malcolm was relieved to have made it to the plane safely, but he knew there would be other confrontations with his former N.O.I. colleagues. The next confrontation came sooner than he expected.

Malcolm was on his way to Chicago to testify before the attorney general of Illinois concerning the activities of the N.O.I. During his three days in Chicago, he was under police guard—and under the angry, watchful eye of the Nation. Black Muslims waited around Malcolm's hotel, followed him whenever he stepped out, and turned up at local a television studio where Malcolm was scheduled to appear on a local program.

During the television program, Malcolm mentioned that various attempts had been made on his life. Later he told a detective, "It's only going to be a matter of time before they catch up with me."

Malcolm arrived back in New York on January 31 and was immediately served with a court order to leave the house in Queens. Malcolm was crushed. "A home is really the only thing I've ever provided Betty since we've been married," he once said to Alex Haley. "[Now] they want to take that away." Malcolm was determined to do better at providing for his family in the future, though he felt that he didn't have much of a future left.

When the court order came, Malcolm called Haley. Malcolm said he planned to appeal the order. Meanwhile, he asked if he could meet with Haley in the coming weeks and look at the nearly completed manuscript of the autobiography. "I just want to read it one more time . . . I don't expect to read it in finished form." Haley agreed to meet Malcolm during the weekend of February 21.

A few days later, on February 4, Malcolm spoke to a gathering of blacks at an African Methodist Episcopal church in Selma, Alabama. The meeting was called as part of a voter-rights campaign organized by the Southern Christian Leadership Conference, the organization headed by Martin Luther King, Jr. King was in jail at the time, and Malcolm had been invited to speak by two members of the Student Non-Violent Coordinating Committee, a civil rights group.

S.C.L.C. officers Andrew Young and Reverend James Bevel asked Malcolm not to "stir up any trouble." Malcolm assured them that he would not.

At the church, Malcolm was seated next to Coretta Scott-King. He leaned toward her and told her that he was there to help. He believed that whites might be more willing to accept King's nonviolent solutions to the race problem once they'd heard his (Malcolm's) militant stance, and he told Coretta as much. Malcolm asked her to let Martin know that he and Malcolm were soldiers in the same war. Coretta never forgot Malcolm's words or his sincerity.

Before leaving Selma, Malcolm mentioned plans to start a southern-based O.A.A.U. Then, on February 5, he flew to London where he addressed the First Congress of the Council of African Organizations. From London he flew to Paris for a scheduled appearance, but French authorities never allowed him to leave the airport. They accused Malcolm of causing violence wherever he went, and told him he was not welcome in France.

Malcolm returned to England to speak at the London School of Economics on February 11. Two days later, Malcolm returned to the U.S.

At 2:46 A.M. on February 14, Malcolm lay in bed asleep with his wife beside him. His daughters slept peacefully nearby in their own rooms. The sound of breaking glass shattered the silence, followed by the loud blast of a fire bomb, and the screams of the children. Malcolm barked out commands. He and Betty snatched the children from their beds and rushed them to the safety of the backyard. The family stood there in the freezing winter night, shivering in robes and pajamas. Betty, pregnant with one child, holding another, waited for the firetrucks that took too long in coming. Malcolm watched the flames leap into the sky as his father had in Lansing, Michigan, all those years ago. Malcolm had never forgotten that night of terror when the Klan burned down his childhood home. Now he was reliving it with his own wife and children. Only this time, Malcolm was convinced, the fire had been started by his own people. He was certain Black Muslims had bombed his house. The thought filled him with rage.

After the bombing, Malcolm took Betty and the children to stay with friends. Once Malcolm felt that his family was safe, he flew to Detroit, where he was scheduled to appear on a television show and to speak at a rally. He had made up his mind long ago that nothing except death would keep him from fulfilling his work.

Malcolm delivered a speech at the Audubon Ballroom in New York the next day, then spoke to an audience at Corn Hill Methodist Church in Rochester, New York. On very little sleep and one meal a day, Malcolm pushed himself from one meeting to the next.

On February 16, Malcolm called Haley to cancel plans to meet the weekend of the twenty-first. He needed time to find a new home for his family and get them moved into it. As a result, he had to rearrange his schedule. That same day Malcolm told a friend, "I have been marked for death in the next five days." If Malcolm was going to find a new home for his family, he had no time to lose.

On the eighteenth, Malcolm went to the burned-out house in Elmhurst, moved the family's personal belongings and stored them at a friend's home. Then he contacted a real estate agent. On Saturday morning, February 20, he and Betty went with the agent to look at houses. They found one they liked in Long Island. Malcolm told the agent that they would probably take the place, and would contact him later. Malcolm drove Betty back to their friend's house.

Malcolm called Alex Haley. Could the publisher give him an advance on the autobiography? Malcolm asked. He needed the money for the down payment on the house. Haley said he'd check into it first thing Monday morning and let Malcolm know.

Malcolm left Betty and the children and drove

downtown to the Hilton Hotel at Rockefeller Center. After the house was bombed, Malcolm didn't dare spend the night with his family. He didn't want to put their lives in danger by being too close for too long.

A few minutes after he arrived at the Hilton Hotel, Black Muslims slipped into the hotel lobby, asking various bellmen what room Malcolm was in. Knowing who Malcolm X was, and that he had received death threats, the bellmen refused to give out his room number. Instead, hotel security was called and Malcolm was warned that men were looking for him. Malcolm went to the hotel dining room for dinner that evening, but otherwise remained locked in his room for the night.

The next morning Malcolm called Betty. He asked her to bring the children to the Audubon Ballroom that afternoon. He would be speaking there at 2 P.M. and wanted the family to hear him. Betty was surprised, since the night before he'd told her not to come to the meeting. Betty didn't argue, though. She said she'd be there and would see him later.

At one o'clock, Malcolm left the hotel and headed for Harlem. He arrived at the Audubon early and sat down offstage until it was time for him to speak. Four hundred seats had been set up for the audience. Malcolm could hear the audience as it filed in.

No one was searched at the door. Malcolm had ended that practice weeks before, saying that it made people uncomfortable and that the searches reminded him too much of Elijah Muhammad.

The meeting was late getting started. By 2:30, the guest speaker, Rev. Milton Galamison, a militant Black Presbyterian Minister known for leading boycotts, had not yet arrived. One of Malcolm's assistants suggested that another member of the O.A.A.U., Benjamin Karim, could open up the meeting as the first speaker in Galamison's place. Glancing nervously at his watch, Malcolm finally agreed. He gave Karim half an hour to speak.

At the end of that half-hour, Galamison still had not arrived. Malcolm was disappointed. He was still finding it difficult to form alliances with other leaders in the black community. Malcolm knew that Galamison would not be coming, though his assistant kept saying, "I'm sure he's just late."

Karim wrapped up his talk and introduced Malcolm. Malcolm stepped out on stage and greeted the audience in his usual way.

"As-Salaam-Alaikum, brothers and sisters!" he said, amid applause.

"Wa-Alaikum-Salaam," said the audience.

Suddenly shotgun blasts tore through the room. People ran for cover, some throwing themselves on the floor, others crouching behind tables. Malcolm reached for his chest as the force of sixteen bullets knocked him to the ground in sight of his wife and children. Betty screamed, shoved her children to the floor and threw her body over them to protect them. When the shots ended, she ran to her husband.

A policeman stationed in front of the Audubon rushed in when he heard the shots. Two other policemen cruising by in their patrol car arrived at the scene as people swarmed out of the ballroom. Several of them were kicking a man who was trying to flee. The two policemen arrested the man and pushed him into their patrol car. The man, Talmadge Hayer, was taken to the police station.

Meanwhile, someone in the crowd had run to the emergency room of Columbia Presbyterian Hospital two blocks away and brought back a stretcher for Malcolm. He was rushed to the hospital and taken to the emergency room. Betty and a crowd of friends anxiously awaited news. Reporters, who were called immediately after the shooting, were also on hand. Finally, a hospital spokesman emerged at 3:35 and made the announcement. "The gentleman you know as Malcolm X is dead."

Malcolm would have been forty years old on his next birthday. His youngest daughters, twins Malaak and Malikah, were born November 5, 1965. They never got to see their father.

Malcolm's body was laid out for public viewing at Harlem's Unity Funeral Home where twenty-two thousand people—black and white—filed past the open coffin to pay their last respects. The name inscribed on the coffin's bronze plate was El-Hajj Malik El-Shabazz.

Upon hearing of Malcolm's murder, police tactical forces were put on alert all over Harlem in case Malcolm's followers went after N.O.I. members for revenge. Mosque Seven was ordered closed temporarily as the city tensed for trouble.

Malcolm's followers found it difficult to locate a church that would hold the funeral. It obviously couldn't be held at any of the N.O.I. mosques. Yet Malcolm was Muslim, and most Christian church officials flatly refused to allow a funeral of someone of another faith to be held on church property. Some churches didn't mind holding a Muslim funeral, but were afraid to get involved because the funeral was for the controversial Malcolm X. As it was, the Unity Funeral Home had received several bomb threats for simply allowing Malcolm's body to be viewed on its premises. Finally, Bishop Alvin A. Childs stepped forward and offered Faith Temple Church of God in Christ as the funeral site. The church, located at 147th Street and Amsterdam Avenue, was in the heart of Malcolm's territory in the days when he was the Harlem hustler named Detroit Red.

Between midnight Friday and dawn Saturday, Malcolm's body was moved to Faith Temple and, by 6 A.M., people had begun to gather outside, forming a line that ran along Amsterdam Avenue. By 9 A.M., the crowd had swelled to about six thousand people. There were seats for six hundred inside the church. The rest of the crowd listened to the service on loudspeakers that hung from the door.

The eulogy was given by black actor Ossie Davis. First, he and his wife, actress Ruby Dee, read cards and telegrams of sympathy that came from major civil rights leaders, most notably Martin Luther King, Jr., and from world leaders such as Dr. Kwame Nkrumah, President of Ghana.

After the telegrams were read, Davis began his eulogy. "Here—at this final hour in this quiet place, Harlem has come to bid farewell to one of its brightest hopes. . . ."

Hope is what Malcolm represented—for black Americans first of all, but finally for all Americans. He was the symbol of hope for the dropout, the drug addict, the criminal, and the bigot—whether black or white. He proved, by example, that change is possible for any American. But first, Malcolm preached, Americans must wake up and face the truth about themselves, and their history of racism. Then they must reach out for the spiritual power to move beyond racism for their own personal good, and the good of the country.

With great passion for his people and a stubborn hope for his country's future, Malcolm X, in his short but powerful life, became an unstoppable force for change.

Epilogue

MALCOLM X, EL-HAJJ Malik El-Shabazz, was buried at Ferncliff Cemetery in Hartsdale, New York.

On March 11, 1965, a grand jury indicted Talmadge Hayer, Norman 3X Butler, and Thomas 15X Johnson for the murder of Malcolm X. Hayer denied having any connection with the N.O.I. While Butler and Johnson were both members of the organization, Johnson being from the ranks of the Fruit of Islam itself.

One year after the trial, the jury found Hayer, Butler and Johnson guilty and the three men were sentenced to life imprisonment. However, many questions remain concerning the assassination.

At the time of the shooting, Elijah Muhammad officially denied that the N.O.I. was involved with Malcolm's murder. One of the convicted men, Hayer, insisted that neither of the other two accused men were involved in the shooting. Malcolm's half sister Ella Collins said that Malcolm had mentioned, weeks before his death, that some of the threats he received might be coming from a government agency, and not from the N.O.I. after all. Alex Haley recorded Malcolm saying something similar to him.

One question that comes up repeatedly is why there weren't more policemen stationed outside the Audubon Ballroom that day. It was widely known that a number of serious threats, and actual attempts, had been made on Malcolm's life. Only a few days before, his home had been fire-bombed. There was certainly cause for an increase in police protection. Instead, police protection was almost nonexistent at the time of the shooting.

As recently as August 1992, Malcolm's eldest daughter, Attilah, who witnessed the assassination, hinted that not all the guilty parties had been brought forward. However, the case remains closed at this time.

Björn Donobauer

About the Author

Nikki Grimes is an award-winning children's book author and
poet. Her articles, essays, poetry, and photographs have appeared in a wide variety of magazines and anthologies. Born
and raised in New York City, she presently lives in California.
Malcolm X is one of her heroes.